HARVESTING PROSPERITY

*Discover Your Freedom to Wealth
Through Life's Lessons*

GILLIAN FOMUM AND CHARLES NDAGHA

Copyright © 2024 Gillian Fomum & Charles Ndagha

All Rights Reserved

Kemp House
152-160 City Road
London, EC1V 2NX
United Kingdom

ISBN: 978-1-9170-0323-0

Published by Gillian Fomum, Charles Ndagha and Action Wealth Publishing.
Printed and bound in the United States

This book or any portion thereof may not be reproduced or used in any manner without the express written permission of the publisher except for the use of brief quotations in a book review.

Although the author and publisher have made every effort to ensure the accuracy and completeness of information contained in this book, we assume no responsibility for errors, inaccuracies, omissions, or any inconsistency herein. Any slights on people, places, or organisations are unintentional.

The material in this book is provided for educational purposes only. No responsibility for loss occasioned to any person or corporate body acting or refraining to act as a result of reading material in this book can be accepted by the author or publisher.

This book is dedicated to our four kids: Gilles, Winner, Keren, and Aldrich. We thank God for you all.

TABLE OF CONTENTS

PREFACE ··· 9
ACKNOWLEDGMENTS ··· 12
INTRODUCTION ··· 15
CHAPTER ONE: GILLIAN'S YOUTH ···························· 18
    Family Lessons ··· 23
    Takeaways from Gillian's Youth ······························ 23
    Educational Years ·· 28
CHAPTER TWO: CHARLES'S YOUTH ·························· 33
    Takeaways from Charles's Youth ···························· 38
    Educational Years ·· 42
CHAPTER THREE: OUR TWO WORLDS IN MARRIAGE · 47
    Takeaways from our Two Worlds in Marriage ············ 56
CHAPTER FOUR: DIVERSIFYING SKILLS OUTSIDE OF FORMAL EDUCATION ·· 67
    How This Benefits Throughout Life ························· 71
    Takeaways from our Two Worlds in Marriage ············ 76
CHAPTER FIVE: HARD WORK IS ESSENTIAL IN LIFE ·· 90
    It Motivates & Rewards ·· 91
    Bosses Who Inspire ·· 91

Wisdom from Daniel Fombo and Gilbert Fon ················92
Geoffrey's Pep Talk ···93
That Extra Push ···93
It Shows Dependability ··96
Gillian ··97
Takeaways from Hard Work is Essential in Life ···········99
Cultural Perspectives on Hard Work ······················ 107

CHAPTER SIX: TRUST IS ESSENTIAL IN LIFE ············ 113
Actions Speak Louder Than Words························· 114
Goal Getter ·· 115
Putting in the Effort ··· 115
Educating and Elevating ······································· 116
Making Targets ·· 116
Success is the Game ··· 117
Always Keep Your Word ·· 118
Being Trustworthy is a Journey, Not an Endpoint ······ 121
Takeaways from Trust is Essential in Life ················ 124

CHAPTER SEVEN: ACCEPTING CHANGE ····················· 138
Accepting Career Changes ···································· 139
Accepting Challenges ··· 144
Takeaways from Accepting Change ······················· 151

CHAPTER EIGHT: THE POWER OF FINANCIAL
LITERACY ·· 159
Building a Secure Future ······································ 160
Leaving a Legacy ·· 164
Our Personal Experiences ····································· 167

An Open Check for Your Legacy ·· 168
Takeaways from the Power of Financial Literacy ········ 169
CHAPTER NINE: HELPING COMMUNITIES ················ 178
How to Do It ··· 180
Creating a Ripple Effect ··································· 185
Be the Change You Wish to See ······················· 186
Takeaways from Helping Communities ··············· 193
CHAPTER TEN: CHANGING MINDSETS THROUGH EDUCATION ·· 203
How it Would Empower Children ······················· 204
Building the Habit of Saving Mentality ················ 207
Breaking the Cycle of Poverty ··························· 209
Takeaways from Changing Mindsets Through Education ·· 214
CHAPTER ELEVEN: EMPOWERING AN ENTREPRENEURIAL SPIRIT ································· 217
Business is Not About the Dollars in Your Account ····· 222
Takeaways from Empowering an Entrepreneurial Spirit ··· 225
CONCLUSION ··· 228
ABOUT THE AUTHORS ·· 232

PREFACE

WE ARE THRILLED to present *Harvesting Prosperity,* a comprehensive and deeply personal narrative that marks our debut in the literary world. This book is not just a compilation of pages; it reflects our life's journey, a tapestry woven from our experiences, struggles, and triumphs. *Harvesting Prosperity* begins by delving into the childhood stories of Gillian and Charles, exploring the intricate details of their backgrounds and the pivotal moments that have shaped their paths to success.

Our book meticulously unpacks the layers of our upbringing, casting light on the impactful experiences that have sculpted our perspectives and values. From the early days of navigating the complexities of family life to the transformative years of our educational pursuits, each chapter is a testament to the resilience and determination that propelled us forward. We share our professional achievements and the lessons learned along the way, hoping that our stories will inspire a shift in mindsets and motivate others to pursue their paths to prosperity.

For those entangled in the intricate web of planning and dreaming of a prosperous future, *Harvesting Prosperity* is a beacon of guidance. This book is crafted to lead you to the wellsprings of success, offering essential insights and strategies in today's ever-evolving world. Our journey underscores the importance of cherishing one's health and well-being as the cornerstone of achieving financial success.

Imagine, for a moment, the figure you would like to see in your bank account. Whether it's thousands, hundreds of thousands, or even millions, this book is about turning that vision into reality. *Harvesting Prosperity* is about understanding and harnessing the principles of financial freedom that allow us to thrive in a world abundant with opportunities. It's about recognizing that the potential for wealth is not just around us but within us, waiting to be unearthed and cultivated.

Join us as we navigate life's rich landscapes, sowing the seeds of knowledge and reaping the rewards of hard work and perseverance. Whether at the beginning of your journey or well on your way, Harvesting Prosperity offers the tools and inspiration to achieve the financial independence and freedom you seek. Welcome to a journey of transformation, empowerment, and abundant success.

ACKNOWLEDGMENTS

FIRST AND FOREMOST, We would like to acknowledge and thank our Almighty God, who has given us the strength and inspiration to share our testimony of the good works He has done in our lives through this piece of work. We appreciate our "clients and business partners who have trusted us to do business together." Your unwavering trust and collaboration have been the cornerstone of our journey, inspiring us to create Harvesting Prosperity. This book is a testament to the myriad experiences we've shared with you and countless families, experiences that have shaped our path from childhood to the present.

The tapestry of our journey into financial professionalism is intricately woven with the contributions of our parents, friends, and acquaintances. From childhood companions to current confidants, each of you has been a divine gift, profoundly influencing our lives. While it's impossible to name everyone, please know that your support is integral to our story and has left an indelible mark on our hearts.

A special acknowledgment is owed to Gilbert Fon, our mentor and guide. His initiative and unwavering focus were instrumental in realizing this dream. His guidance helped transform our vision into a tangible masterpiece; we are eternally grateful.

We also extend our heartfelt thanks to Geffrey Semaganda, our publisher. His expertise in design and dedication to bringing the manuscript to life has turned it into a work of art. His meticulous attention to detail and creative insights have been invaluable in this journey.

Most importantly, we thank our audience for your commitment to safeguarding yourselves and your families. This book is also for those on the cusp of taking that monumental step toward creating a lasting family legacy. Remember, the best time to act is now, as the future is an unfolding mystery. Don't let regret be your refrain when opportunities slip by. The phrase "if I knew" should not be in your story. We urge you to seize the moment, embrace your potential, and harvest your prosperity now. Your journey towards a brighter, more secure future begins with the insights and wisdom in these pages. Thank you for joining us on this remarkable financial enlightenment and empowerment voyage.

INTRODUCTION

Welcome to the exciting world of opportunities, where change is not just a distant ambition but a thrilling validity waiting to be probed. In this book, *Harvesting Prosperity,* we invite you to embark on a lively, amusing expedition loaded with insights that can transform your life. This book's essence is about passing on valuable knowledge, insights, and life lessons. It's a craft for wisdom, a means to enlighten, and a way to preserve those practical insights alive and thriving for future generations.

Through this book, you'll see our lives and an awareness of how change is achievable when we adopt the right mindset. We will share our personal experiences, the limitations we've traversed, and the lessons we've learned on our expedition, desiring that it will illuminate you to seize the opportunities that come your way.

This book examines the mighty power of financial literacy, a mastery that can establish a secure and prosperous fortune. Imagine leaving behind a legacy, an inheritance for your next generation, and a foundation for their success. But that's not all. We'll dig into how, by operating jointly, we can help entire societies rise to new altitudes, creating a ripple impact that touches every corner of society.

Education is the key to unlocking potential. It empowers children, sowing a seed of financial independence, the power to make wise decisions, and the habit of saving for a brighter future. It's enlightenment about breaking the cycle of poverty and sowing the seeds of hope for a more colorful, thriving world.

And then there's the magic of nurturing an entrepreneurial spirit. You see, business is not just about the dollars in your account; it's about the skills, the drive, and the boldness to pursue your visions. It's a pilgrimage that doesn't end with a grade or a job; we will walk you through finance education, a vital ongoing process, and an obligation to lifelong education.

So, as you flip across these pages, get prepared to discover these life-altering lessons and more. Get ready to be encouraged, motivated, and equipped to make change possible and unavoidable. After all, when we work together and share our experiences and proficiency, we develop a world where change is not just a distant fantasy but a vibrant reality. Buckle up as we begin the magnificent adventure!

CHAPTER ONE

GILLIAN'S YOUTH

"He will love the person but strongly dislike the lazy attitude that keeps them from reaching their maximum potential."

—Mathew 25:30

GILLIAN FOMUM WAS a name that echoed through the rolling hills of Efah village in the northwest region of Southern Cameroon. My story began on June 15, 1981, at the Bali Catholic Hospital, nestled in the heart of my homeland. I was born into a bustling household, a home that housed sixteen family members due to the complexities of polygamy.

A strong attachment to my father, a teacher of blessed memory, marked my early years. I was a crybaby, so I found myself changing primary schools frequently. Each time my father was transferred, I had to move along because my constant crying made other schools reluctant to accept me. I just had an insatiable need for my father's presence. I was all about him.

My earliest memory that significantly impacted me was my longing for my father. I grew up in the village of Efah, where life revolved around farming. Despite my father's teaching profession, he deeply loved agriculture. He was both an educator and a farmer. We had numerous coffee farms, and every holiday brought a new task—clearing the farm, tending to the trees, or harvesting the coffee. The money earned from these farming endeavors was crucial to paying our school fees.

These vigorous activities instilled in me the values of self-sufficiency and hard work. Remember, being a child from a polygamous home. I knew the struggle was for me to get something or money for myself because the heavy burden on my parents could be made lighter if I could care for some of my little needs.

In our family, everyone had to participate in all chores, regardless of gender. To us, cooking was a shared task. At a young age, I had a burning desire to make money, even though I was unsure how to spend it. All these were aimed at making sure everyone grows with a level of good practical home training. When I was around ten years old, I would fry groundnuts and sell them to have my savings, and by the time I was 15 years old, I would cook meals and trade them. Though this didn't go well with my dad, I was determined to engage in something to get some money.

While growing up, there were occasions when I had to stretch my limits. I do remember this heart-breaking occasion, which was around 1999, after my dad passed away. I was sent home to get school fees. I felt devastated, and I could not comprehend why they could send me home when the person I looked up to for provision was gone.

At that time, I was full of emotions, and I could not understand why my beloved dad died. I went to the extent of contemplating joining him. But something restrained me from within, and I knew I had to forge ahead despite the challenging situation.

The second challenging moment came when my older sister, who had been helping me, passed away during my advanced-level studies. I questioned the value of life and education. My father was gone, and now the person I thought would guide me was also gone. Everything seemed to fall apart, but I knew I couldn't give up. I needed to push forward, especially when preparing for the advanced level exam, to help me secure a job in the future.

The third occasion was when I aspired to become a soldier and took the entrance exams. During the oral part of the exam, a general made a disgraceful proposition, suggesting that I should meet him in his hotel room to secure a place in the military. He implied I would only make it with his influence even if I passed the exam. I was devastated and heartbroken, that this was a dream I had held onto dearly.

Over the years, there were occasions when some teachers made advances toward me, I refused to yield to their demands and some threw me out of their classes, but their actions ignited my determination more. In such low moments, I found relief from my father's close friend's advice. I fondly remember Mr. John Akum, my late father's freind whom I highly regard for he told me, "My girl, focus on your studies, ignore the detractors, strive, and you will surely excel." These wise words resonated well with me, and during my most challenging times, I'd usually remember his wise counsel. He would tell me, "Cram, pass and forget." Though funny, it reminded me that despite adversity, I had to soldier on, and it became my mantra.

When I look back, I do appreciate these challenging experiences that I went through because they are the ones that have shaped me into the person I am today. Through them, I learned to work hard, be determined, and navigate challenges. As I strive to help others realize the change, my father's memories and Mr. John's wisdom have been my primary sources of guidance.

Family Lessons

My family has always been the pillar guiding the journey of my life. They have instilled in me fundamental principles that have profoundly molded my worldview. My family taught me the value of respecting everyone, the importance of a positive attitude, the value of a family bond, the meaning of decency, and the power of forgiveness. Read on as I share the captivating story behind each deal, making them more meaningful than mere words.

Takeaways from Gillian's Youth

Respect Everyone, No Matter What

Growing up, my parents emphasized the significance of respecting others. They could stress that respect should be accorded to everyone equally, not just those who quickly get along. I recall my mother saying, "Given that you don't know what happened to that person, always remember what happened to them could still happen to you if you don't respect them." That statement hit me hard. It made me realize that showing respect is not just about being polite; it's about understanding that we carry our burdens and stories.

This lesson is like a rock I carry everywhere, as it shapes my interactions with people wherever I am. In this diverse world, this timeless lesson has taught me to continually celebrate nature's diversity and approach each person with an open mind. It's incredible how something as simple as showing respect can profoundly impact your life. When you learn the value of respecting others, you open enormous doors to genuine connections, making meaningful change possible in the most unexpected ways.

Your Attitude Defines You

My parents also instilled in me the idea of being the same person consistently. They implied that the person I was at home should be the same as I am to the world. The aspect of cover-up or pretending to be somebody else was unsustainable, and my parents discouraged me from it. I treasured this advice more, so I began working and interacting with different spheres of people differently.

Over the years, I have learned to appreciate the power of authenticity because it can liberate us. My behavior and attitude have always reflected my personal and professional life. I have always strived to be true to myself and my values without putting on a show, and people have trusted me, which has eventually led to a change in our lives. Through being authentic, I have attracted the right people who have inspired me to work together for a common goal.

The Importance of Family

The family has always been my haven, where I have learned essential life lessons that I have been keen to teach my kids back home. I often tell my kids to be careful of three things: "what you watch, what you do, and what you say." I usually teach my children to respect each other through the family umbrella: "If you don't respect each other at home, you'll continue disrespecting others out there, thinking it's acceptable." I emphasize that the lessons, the values of respect, and the hard work they get from home should be part of their daily lives.

I cherish spending time with family, which is a reminder that the foundation of our character is established at home. Home is where we shape the next generation, teaching them the value of hard work and the vital aspects of respect and decency. Through the precious family moments we spent together, I've witnessed how to sow and nurture the seeds of positive change.

Decency, Dressing and Self-Respect

Dressing decently and respecting myself was a lesson my parents always encouraged me to adhere to at home and outside.

I recall my mom's words: "It doesn't matter what people's opinions are; there is only one person you should always look up to, God."

My mother taught me to question myself and ask, "Is God happy with this? What do the Ten Commandments in the Bible say? Does my dress code align with the Bible?"

These lessons remind me that I should consider my actions and choices in the context of my values and beliefs. In the current generation, it's easy to move with societal norms, but it's crucial to question the trends and check whether they align with your belief system. I become a beacon for others to follow by respecting myself and my values. It's all about upholding a standard and showing the world your value, which is, in turn, reciprocated back to you.

The Power of Forgiveness

It is traditional in my family to emphasize forgiveness. I always tell my kids, "Remember, two wrongs cannot make a right."

If someone hurts you, it's not about retaliating but rather turn and say, "God bless you." This lesson is one of the most challenging yet transformative. It teaches us that change is possible not only within ourselves but also in others.

Responding to hurt with kindness and forgiveness may not reap immediate change in others, but it instills the seeds of transformation. It may take time, but one day, they might sit and reflect on why they're hurting someone who keeps blessing them. This lesson is a powerful reminder that how we respond to negativity can lead to profound change in individuals and society.

These lessons from my family have shown me that when we work together with these values in mind, positive change is not only possible but inevitable. So, let's remember these simple yet impactful lessons and carry them with us as we strive to make the world a better place for everyone.

Educational Years

My education journey was full of ups and downs, but it was the fuel that ignited my passion for nursing. It all began in three different primary schools, each with unique experiences. First, I went to

Government School (GS) Angie, then G S Ogim, and later, G S Ambo, where I got my primary education.

Secondary school life led me to Government High School (GHS) Batibo, a place that shaped my future. I toiled through the rigorous curriculum as from form one to other forms and through high school. Despite the challenges, the road to success is only sometimes smooth; I turned these into my strength, which made me obtain my general education certificate, G.C.E Advanced level. The path to success was laden with obstacles, but I was determined to make my dreams come true. Nursing, a field I deeply cherished, awaited me.

The Catholic Private School of Nursing in Shishong was my next destination—three years of relentless effort and dedication paid off with a nursing diploma in hand. Yet the journey was far from smooth.

There were times when financial difficulties threatened to derail my aspirations. The struggle to pay fees and the stress of exam preparations created overwhelming moments. I vividly remember when the deadlines set for fee payments with exams looming raised the tension more, and it was brought down by my brother, Fomum Sylvester, who had forgone his education to concentrate on poultry farming, which was the primary financial source that sustained me in school. Fomum Athanasius, while still under someone's law chamber, fought tooth and nail for that miracle to happen. It was a heart-pounding race against time, a difficult road I had to walk.

However, by the special grace of God, I managed to navigate these challenges. Those miraculous moments were when fees were paid on the last day, just on time before the exams. It was a testament to my unwavering determination and faith.

Growing up wasn't easy, and frequent battles with malaria made the journey even more challenging. Each bout beat of illness sent me to the hospital, where I found myself hooked up to IV drips. I habitually checked the expiration date on those drips, which earned me curious glances from nurses and doctors.

"Why are you looking at it?" they'd asked.

I just want to read what is on it," I'd say, hiding the real reason. I was merely gaining knowledge, and learning about the tools I aspired to use to care for others.

Becoming a nurse in Cameroon was a dream realized, but life had more surprises in store. My journey took me to America, where my nursing experience in Cameroon was supposed to make the transition easy. However, the reality was different. The evaluation process proved a formidable challenge, and I had to watch my husband pursue his education first while I waited in the wings. Eventually, my credentials were evaluated, and I passed the board exams.

Today, I stand as a nurse in America, a testament to my unwavering determination and the love for caring for others that fueled my journey from those primary schools to the bustling hospitals of a foreign land. This milestone was not a piece of cake because I could hear voices like, you must start school all over in America. With the same determination from childhood, I kept seeking until I got the direction to evaluate my nursing credentials from Cameroon. This led me to achieve my dream of becoming a registered nurse in America. My educational years were a tumultuous path, but they forged the way to fulfilling my dream of caring for others. Descend voices that come your way, and do not allow dream killers to hang around you.

CHAPTER TWO

CHARLES'S YOUTH

"Where there is no struggle, there is no strength."

—Oprah Winfrey

CHARLES NDAGHA IS the name etched into the timeline of a life born on January 13, 1977, in the heart of Cameroon, the Northwest region. My parents, Zacharias Fon (of blessed memory), may he rest in peace, and my ever-resilient mother, Rebecca Tifu, welcomed me. My parents' lives were marked by resilience, determination, and hard work. They toiled relentlessly as peasant farmers to nurture me with an education that would shape my life.

My life was full of indelible memory marks, one of them being the indomitable spirit that my parents had. They showered us with boundless love and relentless pursuit of a better life for us, especially me, which set the pace for my journey. They worked exhausting jobs to make ends meet. Their sacrifices were the foundation upon which I built my dreams and determination to excel academically.

My parent's dedication and unwavering commitment to ensuring I had an education left me with a profound sense of responsibility. I knew I couldn't squander the opportunities they had fought to provide me. Their persistence instilled in me the importance of hard work, pushing me to be a diligent student and ensuring I seized every opportunity to learn and grow. The seed of hard work they planted in me has continued to bear fruit, carrying me from those humble beginnings to where I am today.

I grew up among my nine siblings. Some of the elderly siblings were not with our parents again but with some relatives in Bamenda town, working as house helps. I had to stay with my stepsister, popularly called Ma Rose, from around the late

1980s to the early 90s in Guzang village, a neighboring village. I applaud that experience and appreciate those with whom I grew up together during that segment of my life.

While with my stepsister, it was not all that easy because my father still had to take care of my school fees. This was the moment my direct elder brother, Fon Innocent, had to forgo his secondary education to learn carpentry work, and today, he has that expertise and knowledge even more than some of his peers who learned it in school. This is actually what he used to assist my parents during my secondary and high school days as well as the journey through the years in the Advanced Teacher's Training College. Because of our family numbers, I had to attend secondary school from 1991 instead of 1990 due to financial constraints.

Some occasions were pivotal moments when I had to summon every ounce of perseverance and push myself beyond my boundaries. One of those moments was in 1993 when I encountered a harrowing misfortune. I found myself entangled in a house filled with carbon monoxide, and the circumstances became life-threatening. We were locked inside the house by error, and our chances of survival seemed minimal. Nevertheless, by the grace of God, I came out of that terrifying ordeal alive. The incident served as a potential reminder of the fragility of life and the importance of making every point count. It lit a fire within me—a resolution to keep on and maximize my prospects.

The second model was when I confronted immense financial challenges during my school years. My parents' hard work was pushed to the limit, and there were moments when the finances they could spare weren't enough to fill our necessities, let alone settle for my education. It was a harsh road, but I was unyielding in my willpower. I refused to let financial constraints become a barrier to my dreams. I turned the difficulties into motivation, using them as stepping stones rather than stumbling blocks. Despite the hurdles, I was determined to succeed and pushed myself beyond adversity's limits.

The third significant challenge came when I embarked on the journey to the United States. Leaving behind a career as a secondary school teacher in Cameroon, I faced the daunting prospect of starting afresh in a foreign land. It was far from easy; my path veered into uncharted territories. The opportunities and challenges differed from what I had known, and I had to adapt quickly. My original goal was to continue teaching, but circumstances dictated otherwise. I had to reinvent myself, shifting into health, a field I hadn't envisioned. However, I understood that wherever life ushered me, I had to continue and toil diligently to succeed.

Through these adventures, I have assumed that hard work and perseverance are the cornerstones of advancement. My expedition is a testament to the ability of unwavering allegiance and the enduring essence of resilience. I carry the discourses I learned from my parents, the recollection of that fateful day in 1993, and the challenges I encountered as I worked out a new passage in the United States. These experiences fuel my drive and push me forward, knowing that success results from relentless effort and the refusal to surrender to adversity.

Takeaways from Charles's Youth

Lessons from Family

The bond of family is like a timeless recipe passed down through generations, each ingredient carrying its unique taste and significance. Reflecting on my journey, I realize that my family has been the secret sauce that has flavored my life and career. Our home was a spirited kitchen where the mastery of life was competently cooked, and every task, like a delicious dish, summed up its distinctive seasoning to the blend. In this chapter, I'm enthusiastic to share with you the priceless lessons I've learned from my family, discourses that have not only molded me into the individual I am today but have also been my guiding stars in my nursing profession and financial career. So, let's dive into the pot of our family rites and see how they've enhanced my life.

The Value of Togetherness

Growing up, our family gatherings were like a grand feast for the soul. We understood the significance of being there for one another, and this oration directed me to my nursing career. The notion of being there for someone at their weakest junctures, exclusively like we were there for each other, is something I hold with lots of prestige in my occupation. It's a lesson that reminds me that, jointly, we can make a distinction.

When I resolved to become a nurse, I established that the significance of togetherness was paramount in my family's DNA. We laughed, cried, and stood firm through thick and thin. In my profession, this lesson translates into providing emotional support and being a pillar of strength for my patients. It's the understanding that healing is not just about medication but about the warmth of human connection. My family taught me that, in unity, we can withstand any storm.

The Ethos of Hard Work

At home, there was no room for laziness. From the youngest to the oldest, we all pitched in, be it cooking, cleaning, or doing the laundry. This attitude of hard work has been a cornerstone in my career as a financial professional.

The work ethic instilled by my family taught me that success is the fruit of labor. Just as I witnessed my parents toil tirelessly to provide for the family, I approached my financial endeavors with the same dedication. This commitment to hard work has enabled me to navigate finances, ensuring my clients receive the best possible guidance. The lesson here is that success comes from something other than chance but through dedicated effort.

The Power of Faith

Prayer has been an integral part of our family journey. Seeking God's guidance has shaped my worldview and plays an essential role in my life and career.

Faith is a pillar that supports the roof of our family. Every day, we gather for prayer, not just as a religious ritual but as a reminder that a higher purpose guides us. This translates into making ethical decisions and trusting the process in my financial profession. Our family practice has sowed in me the assumption that it's not merely about the digits but about accomplishing the right thing and trusting that the remainder will follow. The course mirrors my client transactions, stressing trust and principles.

My family has been the compass guiding me through the web of life. They've shown me that together, we can bring about change, that hard work is the foundation of success, and that faith and tradition are like stars guiding us. The lessons from my family are not just pages in the book of my life but the very ink that has written my story. As I balance my roles as a nurse and financial professional, these lessons remind me of the value of compassion, dedication, and integrity in every aspect of my life.

The numerous experiences and emotions I've attained from my family have hardened my life and career, making every day worth an expedition. So, suppose you're wondering how family impacts one's career. The answer is easy: the family's love, importance, and lessons can shape us into the fairest version of ourselves.

Educational Years

My educational journey has been a colorful tapestry woven with threads of opportunity and resilience, starting in Cameroon and leading me to new horizons in the United States. From the dusty paths of my primary school to the hallowed halls of the university, I embarked on a quest for knowledge that has defined my career and worldview.

In the heart of Cameroon, I set foot on the path of formal education. My educational journey began with primary school, where I learned the alphabet, made friends, and discovered the thrill of knowledge. Those early days were a treasure trove of youthful enthusiasm, where the world was painted in vibrant hues with endless possibilities.

High school was the bridge between childhood and adulthood with its tests and challenges. Here, I started to glimpse the vast possibilities that education could open. Each subject added a layer of understanding, from algebra to history, a key to unlocking the world's mysteries.

University life in Cameroon was a whirlwind of academic rigor and social awakening. It was where I began to hone my skills, choose my path, and dream of a brighter future. Those years were marked by friendships that would last a lifetime and professors who ignited the flames of curiosity and ambition.

However, that was not the end. In 2016, I landed in the United States, a new country with new beginnings. And so, in 2018, I resumed my educational pursuits, this time with a different focus. Nursing school became my new challenge, my ticket to a fulfilling career in healthcare.

Yet, it wasn't just the formal education that shaped me. I've always been curious and eager to learn from life. Outside the classroom, I soaked up equally crucial experiences to my development. As I ventured into the working world, the nature of my job opened my eyes to various career paths. Conversations with colleagues sparked ideas and piqued my interest in nursing, ultimately setting me on a new course.

But it wasn't just the professional sphere that taught me valuable lessons. My childhood in Cameroon was filled with experiences that cultivated a strong work ethic. Whether supporting my mum on the farm or assisting my dad in his coffee fields, taping and selling palm wine, these chores were more than duties – they were lifetime lessons that instilled in me the value of devotion and steadfastness. What I witnessed from my parents left an unforgettable mark on me. I understood that hard work was not just a means to an end but a testament to the passion and care they brought into the world for our family.

The sense of achievement I felt when I finished a duty, whether harvesting crops or assisting with household tasks, laid the basis for my work ethic. This determination is what I held with me into my academic and professional ambitions. When I place my hand on something, I confirm it is accomplished to the best of my ability only because God has destined it to happen.

As I traveled through my academic years, from primary school in Cameroon to nursing school in the United States, I maintained the values of hard work, dedication, and an insatiable craving for knowledge. My tale is a testament to the power of schooling and the life sermons that contour us outside the classroom. It's a reminder that the education voyage never ends, and each occasion, each class, is a brushstroke on the canvas of our lives. In all its forms, my schooling has been the compass guiding me toward the transition I wish to build in the world.

CHAPTER THREE

OUR TWO WORLDS IN MARRIAGE

"Time decides who you meet in life, your heart decides who you want in your life, and your behavior decides who stays in your life."

—Tila Mohammed

OUR LOVE STORY began with different melodies, but as time passed, we composed a harmonious symphony of understanding and unity. Our family, a colorful blend of backgrounds and cultures, is a living testament to the remarkable harmony that emerges when we wholeheartedly embrace each other's uniqueness. We're not merely a household but a beautifully intertwined embroidery of customs, values, and imaginations. Our parents sowed in us the priceless virtues of hard-hitting work, discipline, and unwavering faith in God, values that have reinforced the very backbone of our family's muscles.

But here's the kicker: our past lives were as diverse as day and night. It was like navigating two distinct worlds. Yet, our expedition has been a testament to the truth that love has no limits. Our marriage story celebrates acceptance, a rhyme to the beauty of weaving our differences into a harmonious masterpiece of love.

Join us as we dive headfirst into the pleasures and challenges of our multiculturalism union. It's a fable of love, chuckle, and a whole ton of learning. Our pilgrimage is a living, breathing assurance that when we work jointly, change is not only a distant imagination—it's an exciting, ever-evolving tale, waiting to be composed afresh with each passing day."

Gillian

I am married to my wonderful husband, Charles Ndagha, and we are the proud parents of four incredible kids. Let me carry you on an impulsive voyage through our weddings and family life, filled with unanticipated twists and life discourses.

It all began with a chance meeting, the type that only transpires in the movies. My cousin, always the social butterfly, urged me to join him in visiting a friend. I had other plans on that fateful day and almost declined, but destiny had a different script. Instead, my cousin's friend visited our village, where Charles and I crossed paths. Yes, folks, we met in our very own romantic village under the watchful eye of nature.

Our love story unfolded organically. We initiated the talks, and the rest, as they say, is history. Today, we are celebrating 16 years of our union. We celebrated our love with a traditional wedding that was straight out of a Nollywood movie as we registered and signed at the Bamenda II council-Northwest Region Cameroon with family and friends. We danced, sang, and cracked up our way through the celebrations. It was precisely us, our households, and our closest buddies, celebrating a passion bound to survive anything life tossed at us.

Fast ahead to the present, and we are currently parents to a set of boys and girls. Our eldest is a teenager at the ripe age of 15. Then there's a 13-year-old girl who's already making her imprint in seventh grade. Keren, the middle child, is a load of vitality at 10, and our youngest, at 7, keeps us on our toes with his endless interest. They're our pride, joy, and reason for those extra gray hairs.

We might have started with a traditional wedding, but our love story was far from traditional. Charles, a former high school teacher in Cameroon, now juggles a career as a nurse and a financial professional in the United States. Oh, how life has taken us on a wild, unexpected ride! But one sure thing– I never pondered I'd marry a teacher, and guess what? Here I am, entirely obsessed by one.

As parents, we've sought to pass down valuable lessons to our kids, precisely as our parents accomplished for us. We've invested the essence of hard work, instructing them that cooking isn't exclusively a woman's job but a life art. Even our youngest one is learning his way around the kitchen. We've also stressed the significance of respect, not only for elders but for all people. We've ensured they understand the value of spirituality and the need to greet each day with gratitude and humility in God's always-existing presence.

We have taught our children that laziness doesn't usher to success. Whether it's school or job, they've got to give it their all; no shortcuts permitted. Life has its manner of awarding those who prevail and put in the action.

And as for relatives, our story is filled with the support and love of a big, extended family. With 16 members in my family, we've weathered the storms and celebrated the highs together. We've had the privilege of incredible support from my brother, Fomum Sylvester, who went above and beyond to help us through our education. He stepped up when my father passed away and made sure we didn't miss out on schooling. He even paused his education for a decade to ensure we had a chance to excel.

In addition, my other brother, Fomum Anthanasius was of great help alongside other siblings across the country, each with unique stories and experiences that offered unwavering support. More importantly, my family is a patchwork of love, desires, and shared experiences, and we appreciate every instant that has got us to this point. In our expedition, we've discovered that when we toil together, change is not just possible, but it's also magical. Our household is living proof of that, and we wouldn't have it any other way.

Charles

Ah, allow me to tell you about Gillian, the love of my life and the heart of our household. I met her in a tiny village while visiting a buddy, and little did I figure out that this opportunity encounter would alter the route of my life eternally. You see, it's comical how life functions, right? When I came by, I met her, and when I encountered her, everything changed. We began talking and dating, and momentarily enough, we agreed to tie the knot through a simple court union without immense fuss, just the two of us taking a hop of faith alongside our family members and some friends.

We share an indestructible bond. Gillian and I are perfectly the dynamic duo, a crew that's ever in synergy. We've been blessed with four remarkable children, two boys and two girls, who glare up our lives beyond measure. For us, we're not just parents; we're their mentors, their guides, and their friends. We aim to infuse values that mold them into strong, compassionate people.

You'll always see the hustle and bustle of challenging work in our home. Gillian and I work concurrently like a well-oiled engine. We've always been taught that if you want something in life, you've got to work hard for it. I often notify our kids, 'There's no food for the lazy man.' It's a simple fact that we hold special. We want them to determine the value of devotion, perseverance, and the implication of rolling up your sleeves to get things done.

But it's not just about working hard; it's about working smart. We want our kids to face life's challenges head-on, armed with the wisdom and skills to steer any crisis. We want them to grow up with a fear of God in their hearts because that gives life its true purpose and meaning. It's the kind of inspiration that will guide them on the right path as they grow up.

Speaking of values, some gems have been passed down to us from our parents. Trust in God has always been at the forefront. We regard faith as the anchor that retains us leveled, no matter how stormy life's seas may get. That unwavering confidence gives us the stability to face whatever comes our way. As I mentioned earlier, hard work is in our blood.

My older brother, Fon Innocent (popularly known as AZoh), sacrificed his secondary education to learn a trade to support our family. His stubbornness to help us, particularly during my school years, left an unforgettable mark on my job ethic. And then there was my late sister, Ma Rose, who fortified the spirit of hard work in me when I lived with her early in my secondary school years.

In addition to our journey, two business mentors have been our guiding stars. Gilbert Fon and Daniel Fombo are like beacons of light in our lives. They inspire us daily to keep moving forward, no matter how the road seems. Their unwavering backing and encouragement remind us that even in the darkest times, there's always light at the end of the tunnel for those who strive.

So, as I glance back on our expedition and ahead to fate, I can't help but beam. Gillian and I are a living assurance that when we work jointly, change is not just possible but inevitable. Our love, our worth, and the aid of our dear relatives have paved the way for our family's conquest, and we'll keep on moving forward, learning that the journey is invariably worth it. Cheers to life's adventures and the joy of working together!"

Takeaways from our Two Worlds in Marriage

Embrace Diversity in Unity

Gillian and Charles' marriage is a vibrant mosaic of love, resilience, and understanding, beautifully illustrating how differences, when embraced, can become the bedrock of a harmonious and fulfilling relationship. Their story is not just about the union of two individuals but a fusion of diverse cultural backgrounds, values, and perspectives, showcasing the richness that such diversity brings into a relationship.

In their journey, Gillian and Charles have navigated the complexities and challenges of merging different worlds. They have shown that cultural diversity is not a divide but a bridge connecting two hearts in a relationship. Their life together reflects the celebration of each other's unique heritage and traditions while creating a shared narrative enriched by their differences.

This celebration of diversity in unity has not only strengthened their bond but has also provided a vibrant tapestry of experiences for their children.

Their story teaches us that love transcends cultural barriers and traditional norms. It's about understanding and respecting each other's backgrounds, embracing each other's uniqueness, and finding common ground. This approach fosters a more profound connection, mutual respect, and an appreciation for the richness that each partner brings to the relationship.

In today's world, where cultural interactions are increasing every day, Gillian and Charles' journey is a beacon of hope and a model for how love can thrive amidst diversity. It serves as an inspiring example for couples navigating multicultural relationships, demonstrating that with empathy, respect, and open communication, diversity can indeed be a source of unity and strength in a marriage. Theirs is a testament to the fact that when two people are committed to understanding and valuing each other's cultural identities, the resulting union can be an extraordinary fusion of love, learning, and mutual growth.

Importance of Family and Shared Values

The narrative of Gillian and Charles poignantly emphasizes the profound impact of family in sculpting our characters and destinies. Their life story eloquently captures how the foundational values instilled by parents - hard work, discipline, and steadfast faith in God - act as guiding stars, shaping the essence of who we become.

This chapter delves deep into the heart of family dynamics, illustrating how the lessons learned within the familial circle resonate far beyond childhood, echoing into every aspect of adult life. In Gillian and Charles' case, the virtues sown by their parents have become the pillars upon which they built their own family. These values have provided a sense of direction and purpose and fostered unity and resilience in facing life's challenges.

Their story underscores that the family is more than a mere social unit; it's a crucible where essential life values are cultivated and nurtured. The discipline and work ethic instilled in them from a young age have been instrumental in their personal and professional lives, enabling them to navigate the world's complexities with confidence and determination. Equally, their deep-rooted faith has been a source of strength and solace, guiding them through times of uncertainty and reinforcing their commitment to each other and their children.

In today's rapidly changing world, where traditional values often clash with modern ideologies, Gillian and Charles' journey is a testament to the enduring power of family and shared values. It's a vivid reminder that the principles inherited from our families can significantly influence our approach to life, relationships, and challenges.

Their story encourages us to reflect on our family values and recognize their vital role in shaping our individual lives and the fabric of society at large.

Resilience in the Face of Adversity

Gillian and Charles' journey is a profound narrative that exemplifies the essence of resilience. They have encountered and overcome many challenges, from personal losses to the intricacies of building a life within a multicultural framework. Their story vividly illustrates how perseverance, anchored in faith, can turn even the most daunting obstacles into steppingstones toward growth and fulfillment.

This chapter delves into the various adversities they faced, highlighting how each trial shaped their character and fortified their resolve. The loss of loved ones, a challenge that could easily derail many, became an impetus for Gillian and Charles to push forward with incredible determination. Their ability to navigate and integrate differing cultural norms and expectations in their marriage and family life is another testament to their resilience. They have created a harmonious life that respects and celebrates their diverse backgrounds, turning potential conflicts into mutual understanding and growth opportunities.

Their resilience is not merely about enduring hardships but transforming them. It's about adapting and thriving in the face of life's unpredictability. This adaptability is underpinned by a deep-seated faith, which has provided them with a sense of purpose and direction through life's tumultuous journey.

Gillian and Charles' story is an inspiring reminder that resilience is a dynamic process of navigating life's complexities with courage and optimism. It shows that while adversity is an inevitable part of life, the response to these challenges defines the trajectory of one's journey. Their story encourages readers to embrace resilience as a means to withstand adversities and as a path to discovering one's strength, redefining one's purpose, and ultimately leading a more fulfilling life.

Teaching Children Through Example

In *Harvesting Prosperity*, Gillian and Charles' approach to parenting emerges as a robust template for nurturing future generations. Their story beautifully illustrates that teaching children through example is perhaps the most effective form of guidance. By emphasizing values like hard work, respect, and spirituality in their daily lives, they provide a living, breathing example for their children to emulate.

Their parenting style is intensely hands-on, involving active participation in their children's development. This ranges from sharing household chores to instilling a strong work ethic and spiritual grounding. They demonstrate that the lessons imparted to children are most effective when observed in parents' actions. For instance, their shared involvement in cooking breaks traditional gender roles and teaches their children about equality and cooperation.

Moreover, their dedication to hard work is not just told but shown. The children see their parents juggling multiple responsibilities, from managing careers to maintaining a household, which instills in them the value of diligence and perseverance. This approach fosters a sense of responsibility and prepares them to face the challenges of the real world with confidence.

Additionally, the couple's deep spirituality is not merely preached doctrine but a lived practice. This spiritual foundation gives their children a moral compass and a sense of belonging to something greater than themselves. It also instills in them the importance of humility and gratitude.

Gillian and Charles's story is a testament to the fact that the most enduring lessons for children are often those their parents live out. Their life exemplifies that parenting goes beyond providing for material needs; it's about modeling the values and principles children can carry throughout their lives. Through their example, they teach that success in life is not just measured by material achievements but by the strength of one's character and the integrity of one's actions.

The Power of Strong Support Systems

The narrative of Gillian and Charles in *Harvesting Prosperity* vividly illustrates the critical role of solid support systems in navigating life's journey. This chapter delves into the profound impact of supportive networks—comprising family, friends, and mentors—on an individual's personal and professional development. It reinforces the idea that no one achieves success in isolation; instead, it is often the result of encouragement, guidance, and assistance from a community of supporters.

Throughout their story, a robust support system is a recurring theme. For instance, Gillian recounts how her brother, Sylvester, made sacrifices to ensure she could continue her education after their father's passing. This selfless act helped her academically and instilled a sense of determination and responsibility. Similarly, Charles reflects on the support he received from his sister, Ma Rose, and his brother, Fon Innocent, which played a crucial role in shaping his work ethic and resilience.

Moreover, mentors like Gilbert Fon and Daniel Fombo are highlighted as instrumental in guiding them through challenging phases of their lives and careers. These mentors provided advice, motivation, and a belief in their potential, which was essential in their path to success.

This chapter emphasizes that support systems provide more than just emotional comfort; they are a source of practical advice, alternative perspectives, and, sometimes, critical resources needed for growth. These relationships are significant in times of crisis or transition, offering a safety net that can help individuals rebound and continue their pursuit of goals.

The power of strong support systems in *Harvesting Prosperity* reminds us of our interconnected lives. It showcases how the strength, wisdom, and support of others can be leveraged to overcome obstacles, seize opportunities, and achieve success. The chapter encourages readers to acknowledge and nurture their support networks, recognizing them as invaluable assets in their personal and professional journeys.

CHAPTER FOUR

DIVERSIFYING SKILLS OUTSIDE OF FORMAL EDUCATION

"Lazy hands make for poverty, but diligent hands bring wealth."

—Proverbs 10:4

THIS LIFE IS PRECIOUS, with variable lessons to learn each day. It should not be just about vast volumes of textbooks and four-sided classroom lectures. It's a grand carnival of experiences, and it's time to understand the expansive pool of knowledge one can acquire beyond formal education.

Formal education is like your trusty old compass, guiding you through the academic wilderness. But here's the real deal: It's just one piece of the puzzle.

The real magic is unraveled when you step out and attain practical, hands-on crafts.

Think of it as a treasure quest where you're not just hunting for gold but also learning to create a ship to cruise the high seas. Diversifying your skills is like stocking your toolbox with shiny, knowledge-filled tools. It opens doors, creates opportunities, and makes you a more adaptable, resourceful, and resilient explorer of life's grand adventure. So, buckle up and get ready because, in this book, we will unlock the secrets of how diversifying your skills can make change not just possible but fascinating.

Charles

I acquired this skill in my early years and was super proud of it: meeting deadlines on time. It is a priceless soft skill, yet most people take it for granted. It is my nature to be serious and committed to whatever task I handle, ensuring I give it my all. This character I exhibit not only at my place of work but also in everything I tackle. This is a trait I picked up early in life, and I hold it close to my heart.

Back in the day, I had an activity far from the usual 9-to-5 work. I would immerse myself in conversations with people from all walks of life. Those discussions opened my eyes to the extensive array of career options. It was amid these lively chats that I stumbled upon the world of nursing. Sounds random! But it felt like destiny.

Growing up, I had these fantastic opportunities to learn outside of school. I remember accompanying my mom to the farm and witnessing her unwavering commitment. She toiled in the sun, and I knew it was all for our benefit. The same went for my dad's coffee farm. I would join him, coffee beans up to my elbows, and give it my all. That's just the kind of kid I was. I had this insatiable thirst to see things through.

Fast forward, and I'm a nurse now. The journey was wild, but my early love for commitment and my habit of diving headfirst into whatever I do have helped me immensely. So, remember, you never know where your skills might take you. Sometimes, life's best lessons come outside the classroom!

Gillian

Formal education is excellent, but something about learning outside those stuffy classrooms stuck with me. It's like a secret recipe for life; mine revolves around cooking. The great desire I have to prepare those delicious meals, the sweet aroma accompaniments, and the display of the meal on the plate started way back when I was still in school. In our school, we had home economics classes where most figured it was all about aprons and muffins, but to me, it meant much more than that. I enjoyed the lessons of whipping up some delicious dishes and caught that cooking bug.

But the real magic happened at home. My mom was like a culinary architect. She invited people over, and we'd all gather around as she whipped up dishes from different tribes and countries. I was right there, watching, learning, and drooling. Cooking became my passion; I could spot a pro just by watching. I had a culinary sixth sense!

But it wasn't just cooking; it was about rolling up your sleeves and getting your hands dirty. My parents drilled into my head, "No food for lazy men." I'd tag along with folks with skills, whether crafting, fixing things, or farming. They'd show me the strings, and I'd wash it all in.

I do remember the life classes I picked up along the route. My household taught me to keep my environment clean, be punctual, and always be the best wherever I am. It's not something they trained in school for, but it's the wisdom that clings to me.

When I contemplate, I feel proud of the valuable lessons of my learning journey beyond the classroom. Cooking, hard work, and life skills—all rolled into a colorful, flavorful mix—make me who I am today. Cheers to the unofficial curriculum of life!

How This Benefits Throughout Life

These skills have helped us a lot, and we'll lay them out for you: there are and will remain no-nonsense styles that anchor our lives.

Being Punctual

Let's start with the MVP of skills: punctuality. We are those guys who're never fashionably late; We're fashionably early! In this life of hustles and bustles, where time management is a weakness for many, being on time is gold.

It's a skill we learned early and has continued to be our lifesaver. Whether heading to meetings at work, catching up with a flight, or even making a non-official appointment with our friends, we're always on time and ready to roll. We never have to stress about missed opportunities or awkward apologies. We always show up, are present, and do what is needed on time.

Purposeful Action

If you have a purpose that drives your daily activities, your life becomes more manageable and sweeter. Our knack for being purpose-driven has been a guiding light. From choosing our career to making everyday decisions, we're all about "why" and "how." It's like having an inbuilt compass that guides us to where we are going and helps us understand why we're going there. Living a purposeful life has opened many doors, brought us massive success, and made us more confident in our choices.

Determination and Commitment (Charles)

Commitment is something I learned from my parents. I remembered how my mom would take me to the farm. To me, it was like a full-blown mission, no kidding! She'd be out there, laboring her socks off, and I knew it was all for us. That devotion to a cause left an imprint on me. I'd even assist at my father's coffee farm, not because I had to but because I wanted to. That dedication is something I carry in my heart—when I begin something, I see it through.

Cooking Up a Passion (Gillian)

Education brought me some unexpected talents, too. Learning to cook and experimenting with different dishes is like art for me. Watching my mother welcome people to our home and teach them to cook various dishes from other cultures was a new experience. I couldn't help but dive in, and now I can prepare a meal just by watching someone else do it. It's like culinary magic!

Hands-On Learning

The school was one of many places where we soaked up knowledge. We'd get close to people with hands-on skills—the kind of skills not taught in textbooks. Whether it was crafting, woodwork, or even simple home repairs, we'd be right there, eager to learn. It's surprising how these little things add up, and now we can easily handle all sorts of DIY projects.

Running a Tight Ship - Gillian

Speaking of life skills, running a house was never something they taught us in school. My mother gave me a crash course in it. She taught me with a passion to keep my surroundings clean, organize my room, and have everything in order. Now, it has become second nature to me. And let me tell you, it's a rescuer. No more frantically searching for keys or important documents; they have designated spots.

No Excuses, Just Results -Gillian

There's a phrase my mother used to drop like a bomb: "No food for a lazy man." It wasn't an empty threat; it was a personality that molded me and became my way of life. In my family, we all had our respective roles and responsibilities, and if you relaxed off, well, tough luck, friend! It was an assignment of responsibility, and it was waiting for me. If you desire to eat, you've got to toil for it. It was as simple as that!

Reliability and Trustworthiness

The icing on the cake is reliability. When you're known for being punctual, purposeful, and committed, people trust you. Whether it's a group project, a team effort, or just showing up for your family when they need you, you become the go-to person. Its reputation precedes you and has opened countless doors in our lives.

These skills aren't just historical phrases or lessons but our presence's backbone. They've paved the way for successful careers, lifelong passions, and genuine connections with people. Life's too short to be late or unfocused, so we stay committed, purposeful, and always on time. We live by the proclamations we've grasped, and they've never failed us. So, wherever we're, we'll be there on time, prepared to tackle life with determination, commitment, and culinary magic.

Takeaways from our Two Worlds in Marriage

As highlighted in this chapter, the value of Punctuality and Meeting Deadlines delves deep into the significance of these skills beyond their apparent utility. In the professional sphere, punctuality and meeting deadlines are desirable attributes foundational to one's reputation. They signal a sense of responsibility and respect for others' time, which is crucial in building trust and reliability in a work environment.

This reliability can often be the key to career advancement, as it marks someone capable and dependable, ready to take on greater responsibilities.

Beyond professional implications, these skills have a profound impact on personal development. They reflect self-discipline and organization, essential for effectively managing time, prioritizing tasks, and setting achievable goals. This disciplined approach reduces procrastination, leading to a more productive and fulfilling personal life.

Regarding social relationships, being punctual and reliable enhances the quality of interactions. It shows respect for others and helps build stronger, more trusting relationships. Whether in friendships or professional networks, these traits contribute significantly to how individuals are perceived and valued in their social circles.

One less discussed benefit of punctuality and meeting deadlines is stress reduction. Effective time management, a byproduct of these skills, allows for a more relaxed and focused task approach. It eliminates the last-minute rush, often leading to heightened stress and subpar performance. This organized approach ensures better quality work and contributes to a more balanced and less overwhelming lifestyle.

Moreover, consistently being on time and meeting deadlines builds self-confidence. It reinforces an individual's belief in their ability to handle responsibilities and commitments, encouraging a more proactive and positive outlook toward life's challenges and opportunities.

It's also important to recognize the cultural dimensions of punctuality. The importance placed on being on time can vary significantly across cultures. In some, punctuality is a cornerstone of professional and social interactions; in others, there's a more relaxed attitude towards time. Navigating these cultural nuances is crucial, especially in an increasingly globalized world.

Overall, this lesson underscores that punctuality and meeting deadlines are more than mere time management tactics. They are integral to building a reliable and respected persona, enhancing both professional and personal life, reducing stress, and fostering a sense of confidence and competence. These skills, often underestimated, play a critical role in an individual's journey toward success and fulfillment.

Learning Through Hands-on Experience

This underscores the immense value that practical, real-world experiences contribute to personal and professional development. This approach extends far beyond the confines of traditional academic learning. Engaging in hands-on activities such as farming, cooking, or crafting isn't just about acquiring specific skills; it's about immersing oneself in learning processes that are tactile, interactive, and deeply engaging.

These hands-on experiences offer a more comprehensive understanding of the world. For instance, through farming, one not only learns the techniques of cultivation but also develops an appreciation for the complexities of nature and the importance of sustainability. On the other hand, cooking is not just about following recipes; it's an art and science that teaches about different cultures, nutrition, and the chemistry of ingredients. Crafting and other manual skills cultivate an appreciation for the intricacies of design, the value of patience, and the satisfaction of creating something tangible.

Moreover, learning through doing enhances problem-solving skills and creativity. Faced with real-world challenges, individuals learn to think on their feet, innovate, and find solutions. This kind of learning is dynamic and often requires quick adaptation and improvisation, qualities that are immensely valuable in both personal and professional spheres.

Additionally, hands-on experiences often lead to deeper, more memorable learning. Physically engaging in a task can make learning more enjoyable and the knowledge gained more enduring. It also fosters a sense of accomplishment and confidence that theoretical learning alone may not provide.

Furthermore, these experiences can ignite passions and uncover talents that might have remained undiscovered in a traditional classroom setting. They allow individuals to explore various interests and potentially find a calling or career path that is truly fulfilling.

The chapter highlights how hands-on experiences enrich learning by providing a multi-dimensional understanding of subjects, cultivating essential life skills, and opening up new avenues for exploration and discovery. This learning approach encourages acquiring knowledge and its application in practical, impactful ways.

The importance of Commitment and Determination, as illustrated through the stories of Charles and Gillian, reveals how these attributes are vital in navigating life's journey. Commitment and determination are often cultivated through everyday experiences and lessons learned from family, shaping individuals into resilient and goal-oriented beings.

Charles and Gillian's narratives exemplify how commitment - a deep-seated dedication to a task or goal - is crucial in seeing endeavors through to completion. This steadfastness, often instilled in childhood or learned through life's trials, is about more than just sticking to tasks. It's about a consistent dedication to one's values and objectives, regardless of the obstacles. For Charles, this meant learning from the dedication he saw in his parents' work, understanding that genuine commitment involves giving one's best in every situation, whether at work or in personal pursuits.

Determination, closely linked with commitment, is the driving force that keeps individuals pushing forward, even in the face of challenges or setbacks. It's about having the mental fortitude to overcome obstacles and persist in pursuing goals. Gillian's story, for instance, highlights how determination can turn passions, like cooking, into more than just hobbies but significant parts of one's life journey.

These qualities are not just about achieving specific objectives but are essential for overall personal growth. They foster a mindset that is not easily swayed by difficulties or discouragement. Instead, a committed and determined individual is more likely to adapt, learn, and grow from challenges, turning potential setbacks into opportunities for development.

Moreover, commitment and determination are often contagious. When one exhibits these qualities, they set a path for success and inspire those around them. It creates an environment of motivation and resilience, encouraging others to pursue their goals with tenacity.

The chapter underscores commitment and determination foundational to personal, professional, or social success. These qualities enable individuals to remain focused on their goals, persevere through difficulties, and ultimately realize their aspirations. They're the engines that drive progress and the anchors that maintain stability in the turbulent seas of life's challenges.

As discussed in this chapter, Purposeful Action in Life revolves around the profound impact of a clear and meaningful purpose on one's life. It emphasizes how purpose-driven actions can significantly guide individuals in making choices that are not only informed but also deeply fulfilling.

This notion of understanding your 'why' and 'how' is pivotal in providing clarity and direction, ultimately leading to more meaningful achievements.

At the core of purposeful action is understanding one's motivations and intentions. Knowing the 'why' behind your actions gives a sense of meaning and significance to your endeavors. Whether in choosing a career path, nurturing relationships, or pursuing hobbies, having a clear purpose behind these actions ensures that they align with your core values and long-term objectives. This alignment ensures that your path is not just one of success in the traditional sense but also personal fulfillment and satisfaction.

Furthermore, this understanding of purpose empowers individuals to make thoughtful and deliberate decisions. Instead of being swayed by fleeting trends or external pressures, people with a strong sense of purpose can make choices that resonate with their true selves. This leads to a more authentic and genuine way of living, where actions and decisions reflect one's true desires and aspirations.

Additionally, having a clear purpose act as a compass during times of uncertainty or difficulty. It provides a framework for navigating challenges and making tough decisions. When you know your 'why,' it becomes easier to figure out the 'how' – how to overcome obstacles, adapt to changes, and stay true to your course even when the going gets tough.

This concept also highlights the dynamic nature of purpose. As individuals grow and evolve, so do their purposes in life. Recognizing and adapting to these changes is crucial for continued personal growth and fulfillment. It's about being attuned to one's evolving passions, goals, and values and adjusting one's actions accordingly.

The chapter highlights the transformative power of living a life driven by purpose. It's not just about doing things for the sake of doing them but about engaging in actions that have depth and meaning. Purposeful action enriches life, making achievements and milestones of success, as well as personal growth and happiness. It encourages living a life that is not only productive but also deeply rewarding and aligned with one's true essence.

Adaptability and Resourcefulness as essential life skills underscore their critical role in personal and professional development. These traits, often honed through diverse experiences and learning opportunities that extend beyond the bounds of formal education, are vital in equipping individuals to effectively navigate the myriad of challenges and opportunities they encounter throughout life.

Adaptability, the ability to adjust to new conditions and environments, is increasingly vital in today's fast-paced and ever-changing world. It involves an openness to learning and a willingness to modify one's approach in response to new information or changing circumstances.

This flexibility is not just about surviving in a world of constant change but thriving in it. It enables individuals to seize opportunities, pivot in the face of obstacles, and continually grow and evolve personally and professionally.

Resourcefulness, closely linked with adaptability, is about creatively overcoming challenges and maximizing available resources. It's a skill that involves problem-solving, critical thinking, and often, innovative thinking.

Resourceful individuals can find quick and clever ways to overcome difficulties, often when traditional methods or resources are unavailable or insufficient. This ability is invaluable in navigating life's unpredictable paths and turns.

These skills are frequently developed through experiences outside the traditional classroom. Real-world experiences, whether through travel, work, community involvement, or personal projects, provide practical scenarios where individuals must adapt and be resourceful. Such situations foster a hands-on approach to learning and problem-solving, often more impactful and lasting than theoretical knowledge alone.

Moreover, adaptability and resourcefulness are not only about dealing with external challenges; they also involve an internal process of growth and self-discovery.

As individuals adapt and find resourceful solutions, they learn more about their capabilities, preferences, and values. This self-awareness is crucial for personal development and for making life choices that are fulfilling and aligned with one's true self.

Combining these lessons, the chapter presents a holistic learning and personal development approach. It emphasizes the immense value of skills and experiences gained outside formal education. In a world where constant change and uncertainty are given, adaptability and resourcefulness are critical competencies for success and personal fulfillment. They enable individuals to cope with life's demands and actively shape and enjoy their journey.

CHAPTER FIVE

HARD WORK IS ESSENTIAL IN LIFE

"The hard work paid off, and hard work always does."

—Gabby Douglas

IF YOU'VE EVER wondered why your grandma constantly said, "Hard work never killed anyone," or why your coach wailed, "No pain, no gain!" during those backbreaking tasks, you're in the right place.

We're about to untangle life's grand, unshakable fact: Hard work is the secret spice to success. But hey, don't let the term 'hard' shock you away. Think of it as "kick-butt, sweat-soaked, dream-crushing, superhero hard work." We're speaking about the sort of effort that transforms ordinary folks into legends.

In this chapter, we will realize honest conversations about the blood, pains, and tears that make those triumph stories enlightening. We'll show you how challenging work isn't just about bringing in your superior happiness or winning awards; it's about unlocking your full potential, gaining for the stars, and composing your epic tale.

So, get comfy because we're about to launch on a trip that will leave you pumped up, inspired, and ready to conquer life's challenges. Hard work isn't a punishment; it fuels your wildest visions. Let's get this music turned on.

It Motivates & Rewards

Let us share a little secret about motivation and rewards in this crazy life journey. Motivation begins with the people around you, the ones who light that blaze under your butt and hold to burn. So, relax as I take you on a ride through my incidents.

Bosses Who Inspire

In our life, a couple of folks have been like guiding stars for us. First up, our immediate boss. This dude is a legend! He is devoted and sets in the hard work to achieve where he is; it's zero short of inspiring. But it's not just about him crushing away; it's also about how he's always clapping us on. He says, "Hey, you got this! Everybody can make it!" And that, my friends, is the first sprinkle of motivation.

Wisdom from Daniel Fombo and Gilbert Fon

They're like the mentors we all wish we had. They prove that hard work isn't in vain; it pays off! So, when you pour your soul and spirit into your job, it's like a supernatural formula for success. These guys make us believe in ourselves, and their resilience keeps us going, no matter what.

Through their mentorship in financial education through the World Financial Group (WFG) platform, our goal of "no family left behind" is rolling on as many families have been helped to gain financial freedom and create a well of generational wealth-harvesting prosperity.

Geoffrey's Pep Talk

But hold on; there's more to the story. One Saturday, Geoffrey had us all fired up with his words. He said something pierced like an arrow: "If you don't have a story, nobody's going to learn about you."

And that's when it hit us like a bolt of lightning. It's all about developing your narrative, your legend. You see, it's not just about laboring hard; it's about sharing your journey with the world. That's where the actual work transpires.

That Extra Push

Geoffrey's words lit a fire in our belly, still burning. We've got this newfound interest in the field like we've been given a double shot of motivation. Knowing that everything is possible, that's some powerful stuff right there.

Motivation: it's like a team sport. You've got these amazing people around you, propelling you forward, which brings you through the toil. But remember, it's not just about working hard; it's about sharing your tale and exhibiting what you're made of to the world. So, take a page from Gilbert Fon, Daniel Fombo, and Geoffrey's playbook – keep grinding, stay inspired, and let your story shine. That's the secret sauce to making it in this wild ride we call life. This is why our story will keep on numbering pages as we continue educating families on financial freedom. *It Shows Commitment*

Let us tell you a story about how hard work and commitment became our superpower in finance. It all started with some influential people who gave us the kick we needed to take off.

Our mentor is like a 24/7 hotline, always there when we need him. He'd pick up our calls and answer our questions, and even if he missed our call, he'd call us back ASAP. That's dedication right there.

Hard work and devotion go hand in hand. It's not merely about chatting but about seizing the opportunity to take action, putting in the hours, and never giving up.

So, next time someone tells you no, remember it's just a matter of time. Keep moving, keep improving, and sooner or later, you will have the success you are working so hard for.

Hard work is often seen as a measure of one's commitment to achieving success. This is because success is rarely achieved without effort and persistence. When an individual is willing to put in the time, energy, and sacrifice necessary to reach their goals, it shows a dedication and determination that is admirable, and hard work is often seen as a tangible manifestation of commitment, particularly when striving for success. It's the physical and mental effort we put into achieving our goals, and it stands as a testament to our dedication and perseverance.

When working hard, people actively invest time and energy into reaching their objectives. This shows deep commitment because they will sacrifice immediate comfort for future gain. It's a testament to their belief in the value of their goals and their resolve to achieve them.

Moreover, hard work often involves overcoming challenges and setbacks. The ability to persist despite difficulties is a strong indicator of commitment. It shows that the individual is not easily deterred and is willing to push through adversity to pursue their vision.

It's not just about putting in intense effort in short bursts but maintaining a steady, disciplined approach over time. This consistent effort is a clear sign of commitment, indicating that the individual is prepared to stay the course no matter how long it takes.

It Shows Dependability

In Cameroon, where we hail from, we have a saying: "When a woman is pregnant, that baby is yours, but when you put to birth , it's the whole village's responsibility to raise that child." This means that everyone pitches in to ensure the child grows up well, whether financially, educationally, or spiritually.

So, if we can provide for someone's education, it's like helping them out. And now that we've ventured out here, folks back home think life in America is all rosy, but they aren't seeing any pots of gold. That's when we realized that our hard work positively impacts us and our families and can make a difference in our community.

Here are some steps to catch up with the "professional" dress code. We're all about our traditional wraps and cultural attire from back home. But these folks always insist on the whole professional getup. It's a cultural clash, and we miss our comfy wrappers!

Gillian

So, this financial professional gig came into my life, thanks to my husband, who got into it first. However, they didn't explain it to him all that well. When I got wind of it and brought it up to my "king," he was all ears. I asked him to do a policy for me, thinking it could work wonders.

I told him, "Hey, while I'm hitting the books, you can give it a shot."

He was thrilled at the prospect because he knew it could give us more quality time together like we used to have. Now that I'm out working most of the time, he's my go-to guy for handling online stuff, from booking flights for my business trips to arranging Ubers when I'm out of state. He's always got my back!

And you know what he keeps saying to me? "You can do it." That phrase keeps me going, reminding me that hard work isn't just about the sweat and grind; it's about showing dependability to those you care about. It's about carrying your community on your shoulders, even if it means occasionally swapping your comfy wraps for a professional suit.

Nevertheless, I am working hard for myself, my loved ones, and folks back in Batibo, ensuring we all grow together. And I'm lucky to have a partner who believes in me and pushes me to keep going. Yep, life is better when you've got dependable people by your side!

Takeaways from Hard Work is Essential in Life

Motivation and Rewards from Hard Work

A deep connection is established between the effort we put into our endeavors and the motivation that drives this effort, leading to the rewards we ultimately reap. The chapter underscores the significance of having inspiring figures around us, such as mentors and leaders, who serve as role models and actively encourage and motivate us. Their influence is key to how we perceive and engage in hard work.

When bosses demonstrate dedication and commitment through their actions or mentors impart valuable wisdom, they set a standard for us to aspire to. These figures become benchmarks of what can be achieved through persistent effort. Their examples show us the heights that can be reached by embracing hard work. This sort of leadership is not just about guiding or instructing; it's about inspiring through action.

Moreover, these role models help us recognize the value of our hard work. Often, in the grind of daily tasks, the significance of what we are working towards can become obscured. Inspirational figures help keep our goals focused, reminding us why we are putting in the effort and what we aim to achieve. This clarity is crucial as it aligns our efforts with our objectives, making our work more purposeful and directed.

The motivation stemming from such leadership and guidance is a powerful force. It fuels our drive and determination, making the hard work feel less like a burden and more like a meaningful journey toward a worthwhile goal. This intrinsic motivation is important because it sustains us through challenges and setbacks. Our resilience and capacity to persevere are significantly enhanced when motivated by internal factors like personal growth, satisfaction, and pursuing specific goals.

Furthermore, when they come, the rewards of hard work are not just external achievements like promotions, accolades, or financial gain. They also include personal satisfaction and the sense of accomplishment from meeting and surpassing challenges. These rewards are often more fulfilling because they are not just about what we have achieved but about who we have become.

This chapter illuminates the cyclical nature of hard work, motivation, and rewards. The people who inspire us fuel our motivation, which drives us to engage in hard work. This hard work leads to various bonuses, further motivating us and others. It's a dynamic process where each element feeds into and enhances the others, creating a continuous loop of effort, inspiration, and achievement.

Demonstration of Commitment through Hard Work

Eloquently articulates how hard work is a tangible manifestation of one's dedication to a goal or endeavor. This concept is illustrated through personal narratives that bring to life the idea that diligently applying oneself is a clear and visible sign of commitment.

In any professional setting, hard work is often immediately noticeable. It's reflected in the quality of the work, attention to detail, and willingness to go above and beyond what is required. For instance, an employee who consistently stays late to ensure a project meets its highest potential or a team leader who invests extra hours mentoring and supporting their team demonstrates a solid commitment to their role and the organization's success. This consistent effort is recognized and valued as it contributes significantly to achieving collective goals.

Similarly, in personal endeavors, commitment through hard work is equally apparent. Whether it's someone training for a marathon, mastering a new skill, or building a passion project, the consistent effort and time they invest are direct indicators of their dedication. These pursuits often require balancing with other life responsibilities, making the commitment even more pronounced.

Moreover, this commitment is often a prerequisite for success. Success, in most cases, doesn't come overnight but results from sustained hard work over time. This process involves the physical act of working, planning, strategizing, and continuously learning and adapting. It's about steadfastly pursuing a goal, even in the face of challenges and setbacks.

The personal stories highlighted in the chapter serve to underscore this point. They show that hard work is more than just a series of actions; it's a mindset. It's about having a clear vision of what one wants to achieve and being willing to put in the effort required. This dedication often separates those who achieve their goals from those who don't.

Furthermore, the chapter emphasizes that commitment through hard work is about achieving personal success and setting an example for others.

It inspires and motivates those around us, creating a culture of dedication and excellence.

In summary, the chapter beautifully conveys that hard work is a clear demonstration of commitment, both in professional and personal realms. It shows that success is not just about talent or opportunity but largely depends on the willingness to work hard and consistently commit to one's goals. This commitment is a journey of personal fulfillment and a powerful tool for inspiring others.

Dependability Showcased by Consistent Effort

This highlights how dependability is deeply rooted in consistently applying hard work. Through real-life examples, the chapter demonstrates that hard work transcends the realm of personal achievement and extends into the sphere of communal and relational well-being.

Dependability, as portrayed in the chapter, is about being a reliable force in whatever capacity one serves, professionally or personally. In a professional context, an individual who consistently delivers quality work on time and tackles challenges head-on becomes a pillar of dependability.

Colleagues, leaders, and clients come to rely on this person not just for their skill but for their unwavering commitment to meeting and exceeding expectations. This reliability forms the foundation of trust, essential in any professional relationship. It fosters a sense of security and stability, knowing that there is someone who can be counted on, even in challenging circumstances.

In a personal context, dependability is equally, if not more, vital. The chapter illustrates this through stories of individuals who, through their consistent efforts, contribute significantly to their families, partnerships, or communities. This could manifest in various forms - a family member who always provides support, a friend who's there in times of need, or a community member who actively participates in communal activities. Repeated over time, these actions establish a person as a dependable figure in their circles.

Furthermore, the chapter emphasizes that this dependability, born from hard work, has a broader impact. It's not just about the benefits gained but also about the positive influence exerted on others. Dependable individuals often inspire those around them to strive for reliability and consistency in their endeavors. They set a standard of excellence and commitment that can elevate the entire group, be it a family, a team, or a community.

Moreover, in relationships, whether personal or professional, dependability strengthens bonds. Knowing they can count on someone builds a more profound sense of trust and mutual respect. This trust is fundamental to strong, lasting relationships. It creates a supportive environment where all parties feel valued and understood, leading to more effective collaboration and deeper emotional connections.

In essence, the chapter sheds light on how consistent hard work is a key indicator of dependability. It shows that being dependable is more than just showing up; it's about contributing meaningfully and reliably over time, strengthening relationships, and fostering a sense of community and mutual support. This dependability is invaluable in creating a stable, trusting, and supportive environment in one's personal life and professional endeavors.

Cultural Perspectives on Hard Work

How worldwide cultures perceive and value hard work. It highlights that the concept of hard work is not monolithic but is interpreted and embraced differently across various cultural contexts. These differences are not just in the attitude towards work but also in how work is integrated into one's life, the balance between work and other aspects of life, and even in the outward expressions of professionalism, such as attire.

One striking example discussed in the chapter is the contrast in dress codes. In some cultures, attire like suits and formal wear is a hallmark of professionalism and hard work. It symbolizes dedication, seriousness, and a commitment to one's role. This perspective is often prevalent in Western corporate environments where professional attire has a distinct uniformity, reflecting a broader cultural emphasis on formality, structure, and uniformity in the professional setting.

In contrast, other cultures may place less emphasis on formal attire as an indicator of hard work and professionalism. For instance, traditional or cultural attire might be more accepted and professionally valued. This approach reflects different values where personal identity, cultural heritage, and comfort may be prioritized over formal presentation. It illustrates that professionalism and hard work are not defined solely by outward appearance but can be demonstrated through actions, quality of work, and dedication.

The chapter further explores how these cultural nuances extend beyond attire to aspects like work-life balance, attitudes toward time management, and hierarchical structures in the workplace. In some cultures, long hours and sacrificing personal time for work might be seen as a sign of dedication and hard work. Maintaining a healthy balance between work and personal life is considered equally important, reflecting a belief that rest and personal well-being are crucial for long-term productivity and success.

Understanding these cultural perspectives on hard work is crucial in today's globalized world. It fosters mutual respect, enhances cross-cultural communication, and helps create inclusive work environments. Recognizing that there are multiple ways to demonstrate hard work and professionalism allows for a more holistic appreciation of the diverse workforce. It encourages us to look beyond our cultural norms and understand the varied ways in which commitment, dedication, and professionalism can be expressed and valued.

In summary, the chapter acknowledges and celebrates the diversity in the global workforce. It encourages an open-minded approach to understanding different cultural attitudes towards hard work and professionalism, advocating for a broader, more inclusive perspective on what it means to be a hardworking and dedicated professional in a multicultural world.

Hard Work as a Path to Personal Growth and Community Development, the narrative expands the understanding of hard work beyond the pursuit of individual success. It portrays hard work as a significant contributor to personal development and vital in fostering community growth and prosperity. This broader perspective transforms the concept of hard work from a means to achieve personal goals to a powerful tool that benefits the larger society.

One of the key themes is how hard work contributes to personal growth. Engaging in diligent work isn't just about accomplishing tasks or reaching personal milestones; it's also about the learning and development that occurs in the process. Through hard work, individuals learn new skills, develop resilience, and better understand their strengths and weaknesses. This process of self-improvement and personal development is continuous and multifaceted, encompassing professional skills and personal attributes like discipline, patience, and perseverance.

Moreover, the chapter emphasizes the communal aspect of hard work. When individuals work hard, they don't just benefit themselves; they contribute to the welfare and advancement of their community. For example, entrepreneurs who work tirelessly not only create successful businesses but also generate employment, drive innovation, and contribute to the economy. Similarly, individuals who dedicate themselves to public service or community projects help to build stronger, more resilient communities.

This perspective of hard work also includes giving back and sharing success. It's about using one's achievements and experiences to uplift and support others. This could be through mentorship, community service, philanthropy, or being a positive role model. By doing so, the benefits of hard work extend beyond the individual, creating a ripple effect of community growth, development, and empowerment.

Furthermore, the chapter suggests that when communities recognize and value the hard work of their members, it creates an environment of mutual support and shared prosperity. This communal appreciation of hard work fosters a culture of collaboration, respect, and collective advancement.

In conclusion, this chapter redefines hard work as a pathway to personal achievement and the broader goal of community development. It underscores the idea that hard work is not just an individual endeavor but a communal asset with the power to transform societies and improve lives. This holistic view of hard work highlights its role as a fundamental aspect of a fulfilling and meaningful life, both for the individual and the community.

CHAPTER SIX

TRUST IS ESSENTIAL IN LIFE

"The best way to find out if you can trust somebody is to trust them."

—Ernest Hemingway

TRUST IS A FUNDAMENTAL principle that guides us through the web of existence. Being truthful and trusting in what you do can be a game-changer.

Remember what Grandma always said? "Honesty is the best policy." Well, that's the ticket! The principle is to be truthful, and it's like the secret sauce that makes the trust sandwich utterly delicious. We'll unpack how this simple but mighty concept can make your life smoother.

Learning isn't just about acquiring knowledge; it's a recipe for success. It's like seasoning your trust sandwich with flavors you never knew existed. When you learn more, you give more, and the output? It's tremendous!

As we venture into the world of trust, truthfulness, and the insatiable hunger for knowledge. We'll uncover how this magical trio can transform your life into something utterly fantastic. And as a reward for being sure of what you're doing.

Actions Speak Louder Than Words

"Actions speak louder than words!" It's a little saying we've always lived by.

When we set our eyes on a goal, we don't just want to speak about it; we want to make things happen. It's all about that sweet flavor of triumph at the end of the lane. Whether it's a new venture or just a simple conversation with someone, we're all in, giving it our best shot.

As an action fellow, we ensure we implement the following strategies.

Goal Getter

This is our trick: we set a goal, and we're like a heat-seeking missile. No kidding! We don't just throw away the idea; we roll up our sleeves and dive right in.

If it's a business venture, it's not just about saying, "We want to make this work," we're not the ones to pose around and wait for miracles; we make our fortune as we take the giant step toward financial freedom.

The fight against poverty cannot be postponed for your children, but must be won by you.

Putting in the Effort

Here's the secret – effort. If you want something, you've got to hustle for it. No shortcuts, no excuses. For us, we pour all our energy into what we do. It's like we've got this endless fuel tank of determination by giving it everything we have!

That is why the phrase "no family left behind" will always surface at any point in this financial education process.

Educating and Elevating

We have this style when talking to someone; we don't merely nod and smile. We take it a notch higher. We desire to educate, elevate, and motivate. If we understand something that can benefit another person, we share it. We're like a walking, chatting knowledge dispenser.

It's not just about knowing; it's about passing it on and enabling someone else to thrive. It is often said one can be in a river but can still complain of lack of water to watch his face. As immigrants, we have to create generational wealth by getting an account that will take care of us in case we cannot go to work. Do you believe you can get richer even when you are sick of critical, chronic, or terminal illness? Why not become a business owner?

Making Targets

Targets are our best friend. When we set our mind to do something, we don't simply aim for it; we go for it until we succeed. Whether it's a personal goal, a business milestone, or even a small task, we treat it like a big deal.

Our target is our mission, and we'll do our best to achieve it, leaving no room for messing around! The decision was taken already, with evidence being the more than ten policies or index universal life (IUL) accounts we have for a family of six while prospecting to have more because of the importance we have seen and witnessed people benefit from them.

Success is the Game

We have a principle where we don't do things for the sake of it; we do them to see tangible success. For us, it's not about empty words. It's about concrete achievements. Success is the beam of light at the end of the tunnel.

In the end, the grand thing to emphasize is that – actions speak louder than words. It's not about what you say but what you do. When we set a goal, we will not just talk about it; we will work for it. We will hustle, educate, and make it to the finish line.

That's how we roll. Next time you've got that project, don't just sit and chat about it - take action.

Put in the effort, educate, set targets, and go for that sweet success. Words are nice, but moves, well, they're what make things happen! The extension to others has led to many families multiplying their IUL accounts to protect themselves and their families.

Always Keep Your Word

We live by this simple saying, "Always keep your word," Which has impacted the world around us. We're optimistic about this vision for the future, a concept about less hard work and more financial freedom that can turn those dreams into reality.

To achieve this, we require a fundamental principle: mind the power. In Cameroon, our community has these mindsets, which we call old-school thinking, holding them back. But there is a secret – we can change that, and the tool we need is education. It's not a one-time gig, no! We must keep talking, just like that good old Bible says – knock, and the door shall be opened; seek, and you shall find. Our mission is to keep on knocking and seeking. It has been a journey of chiseling this mindset, one conversation at a time.

You may ask why this is so important. Well, because in our community, some folks can be a tad stubborn. You show them something you believe in and know can improve their lives, but they're all like, "Nah, we're good for now." Trust us, we have been there, and we heard that. But the truth is – they might not see it today, but they'll need it tomorrow. It's like they've got these shades on, and they can't see the bright future we're trying to paint for them.

That's where the "always keep your word" mantra comes into play. You must stick to your guns when you promise something and say you'll do it. That's how trust is built. When you keep your word, people begin to believe in you. They see that you're not all talk, no action. You're the real deal, the one who walks the walk.

Our community has had its fair share of hiccups and stumbles where some folks don't learn from past mistakes. But we're not giving up; we're determined to change that. We're showing them that history doesn't have to repeat itself, that we can break the cycle, and we have a game plan: We will keep talking, knocking, and seeking.

We're going to change those mindsets one conversation at a time. And, most importantly, we will keep our word every single time. Because when you always keep your word, you become a beacon of trust and reliability in a world that sorely needs it.

A picture in mind of less hardship and better financial freedom is not just a pipe dream but a destination we can reach. Let's roll up our sleeves, let's keep on knocking, and let's always, always keep our word. Together, we can make that vision a reality!

Being Trustworthy is a Journey, Not an Endpoint

Being trustworthy is like a never-ending journey, not a destination. We've learned this first-hand, and it all started when we moved from Cameroon to the land of opportunity – America! And it is our nature to itch to share the good stuff.

We can't help but spread the word if we stumble upon something marvelous. Back in my motherland, Cameroon, it felt like people were allergic to encouragement and good vibes. We would try to share something good, and they'd hit us with the "You can't do it" speech.

It was frustrating; for instance, when I (Gillian) became a nurse, you'd think I was trying to climb Mount Everest barefoot. All I heard was, "You can't do it."

But guess what? I knew I could! So, I faced the challenges head-on. I did it. I became a licensed nurse in America, and that's when it hit me – I could use my experience to inspire others. My journey wasn't just for me; it was a beacon for anyone who dared to dream. !

On becoming a financial professional, we noticed a common thread among us Africans – we love to talk about our dreams and plans, but when it comes to putting our money where our mouths are, it's a whole different story. We'd chat about what we'd like to do, like, "When I pass away, I want this and that," but when you asked if they've got their finances in order, you'd draw a blank.

This is a classic case of "talk is cheap." That's when we realized that the world is brimming with incredible information, but sometimes, it's like a best-kept secret. So, we made it our mission to be the prophet of goodness. If we found something fantastic, we'd share it. It didn't matter if not everyone got on board – those who listened and paid attention would be the real winners. Our philosophy is simple – don't hoard the good stuff! Don't let it collect dust in your mind if you've got a nugget of wisdom, an exciting discovery, or a heartwarming story. Please share it with the world!

But here is the fact: only some things you think are fantastic will be seen as excellent by others. It's like trying to convince someone that pineapple belongs on pizza – not everyone will buy it. But you never know when a tiny piece of wisdom might turn someone's life around or make their day brighter. In this never-ending journey of being trustworthy, we've realized that trust isn't just about reliability; it's also about sharing, caring, and giving. It's about being the messenger of positivity, the deliverer of knowledge, and the ambassador of good vibes.

You should keep sharing the good stuff, even if not everyone is on board. Trust that your enthusiasm and the seeds of goodness you sow will find fertile ground. You might change someone's life or make their day!

Takeaways from Trust is Essential in Life

Actions Speak Louder Than Words

This part of the chapter delves into the crucial concept that absolute integrity and trust are demonstrated through actions, not just verbal commitments or promises. This principle is foundational in personal and professional realms and pivotal in building and sustaining trust.

When individuals set goals, their actions toward achieving these goals genuinely speak to their commitment and integrity. For example, employees might express their intention to complete a project or improve a skill professionally. However, their actual effort in working towards these goals—staying late to finish the project, actively seeking feedback, and enrolling in courses for skill improvement—truly demonstrates their dedication. Such actions solidify their reputation as a reliable and committed individual.

Similarly, trust is built and maintained in personal relationships through promises and consistent actions that align with those promises. For instance, a friend who offers support in difficult times and follows through with their offer is perceived as more trustworthy than one who makes empty promises. Actions, in this context, prove the sincerity of their words, thereby strengthening the bonds of trust.

This principle also extends to leadership. Leaders who set visions and goals and actively work alongside their team to achieve them are often more respected and trusted. Their actions serve as a powerful model for their team, instilling a culture of accountability and integrity.

Moreover, the chapter emphasizes that this approach leads to tangible personal achievements. When actions align with words, goals are more likely to be achieved. This alignment ensures that efforts are focused and consistent, critical factors in realizing success in any endeavor.

In essence, the maxim that actions speak louder than words is about embodying the values and commitments one professes. It's about being a person of action, where equally resolute and consistent deeds match promises and words. This approach leads to personal achievements and solidifies trust in various relationships, making it a cornerstone of personal integrity and professional reliability.

"Always Keep Your Word" highlights the profound impact of promises on building and maintaining trust. This tenet is crucial in all aspects of life, from personal relationships to professional interactions. In the context of evolving from traditional or 'old-school' thinking to embracing new possibilities and mindsets, keeping one's word becomes even more pivotal.

Keeping one's word is essentially about demonstrating reliability and commitment. When an individual consistently fulfills their promises, they are dependable and trustworthy. This reliability is the foundation of solid relationships. In personal settings, whether with family, friends, or partners, keeping promises strengthens bonds and creates a sense of security and mutual respect. People know they can count on the individual, deepening the relationship and fostering a supportive environment.

In professional contexts, keeping your word is equally important. It can range from meeting deadlines to upholding business agreements or following through on commitments made to colleagues and clients. In such settings, reliability is a personal attribute and a professional necessity. It enhances one's reputation and often opens doors to new opportunities and collaborations, as people prefer to work with trustworthy individuals.

Moreover, in communities where skepticism or mistrust is prevalent, perhaps due to past experiences or cultural norms, consistently keeping one's word can be transformative. It can break cycles of doubt and build new foundations of trust. Demonstrating that one can rely upon challenges and change existing perceptions allows for more positive and constructive interactions.

This principle of keeping your word also plays a critical role in leadership. Leaders who stand by their commitments inspire trust and respect from their team members.

This trust is crucial for effective leadership, as it encourages openness, cooperation, and a sense of collective purpose.

Furthermore, keeping your word is not just about the big promises; it's also about the small commitments made daily. These small acts of reliability accumulate over time, contributing significantly to one's overall character and reputation.

In summary, the chapter "Always Keep Your Word" encapsulates the essence of trustworthiness. It underscores that being a person of your word is critical to building trust in personal relationships, professional settings, or community interactions. This principle is essential in fostering a reliable, respectful, and trustworthy environment for personal growth, professional success, and community development.

Being Trustworthy is a Journey, Not an Endpoint
Trustworthiness is portrayed not as a static quality but as a dynamic, ongoing process. The narrative draws upon the experiences of immigrants adapting to a new culture to illustrate the complexities and continual nature of building trust.

The journey of immigration is a powerful metaphor for the evolving nature of trustworthiness. Immigrants often face the daunting task of establishing themselves in a new environment where cultural norms, social expectations, and even the basic rules of engagement can vastly differ from what they're accustomed to. In this context, trustworthiness is developed over time through consistent actions and interactions.

Being trustworthy in a new cultural setting involves continuously sharing knowledge and experiences and maintaining a positive outlook. It's about more than just avoiding falsehoods or deceit; it's about meaningfully contributing to the community. For example, immigrants might share their unique cultural perspectives or skills, enhancing the cultural richness of their new community. They might volunteer in community services or participate in local events, demonstrating their commitment and reliability.

Moreover, trustworthiness is also about being a source of inspiration and support for others, which is particularly poignant in the context of immigration. Immigrants often find themselves in positions where they can offer unique insights and encouragement to others facing similar challenges. They can inspire others and help foster a supportive environment by sharing their stories of adaptation and resilience.

This process of building trust is iterative and reciprocal. As immigrants integrate into their new communities, their consistent demonstrations of trustworthiness not only help them to form strong, trust-based relationships but also enable the community to grow more welcoming and inclusive.

The chapter emphasizes that trustworthiness is not about reaching a final state where no further effort is required. Instead, it's about continually engaging in actions that reinforce and reaffirm one's reliability and integrity. This ongoing journey strengthens trust in personal, professional, or community-oriented relationships.

In summary, the chapter presents trustworthiness as a journey involving continuous effort, adaptation, and sharing oneself with others. It is a dynamic process that evolves with each interaction and is especially poignant in adapting to new cultures and environments. This perspective underscores the importance of ongoing efforts in building and sustaining trust in various aspects of life.

The Power of Sharing Knowledge and Positivity

This emphasizes sharing information and maintaining a positive outlook in building and reinforcing trust. This dissemination process is not just about imparting knowledge but about fostering an environment of trust and goodwill, strengthening communal bonds and individual relationships.

Sharing knowledge is a powerful way to establish oneself as a trustworthy individual. When someone consistently provides valuable and accurate information, whether professional expertise, practical advice, or insightful wisdom, they become a go-to source in their community or network. This reliability in providing knowledge builds a reputation of being informed and dependable, a cornerstone of trust.

Moreover, sharing information is often seen as a gesture of goodwill. It demonstrates a willingness to help others grow and succeed, a trait of a collaborative and supportive individual. This benefits the recipients of the knowledge and enhances the sharer's sense of self-worth and fulfillment, knowing they are contributing positively to the lives of others.

The chapter also highlights the importance of maintaining a positive attitude in trust-building. Positivity can be infectious, and by consistently projecting an optimistic and encouraging demeanor, individuals can foster an environment of hope and resilience. This approach is particularly impactful in challenging situations, where a positive outlook can be a beacon of support and reassurance.

In addition to sharing knowledge and positivity, storytelling is a powerful tool for trust-building. Uplifting stories and personal experiences, especially those that involve overcoming challenges or learning important life lessons, can be incredibly inspiring. They offer practical insights and humanize the sharer, making them more relatable and trustworthy.

Sharing knowledge and positivity also involves active listening and empathy. It's about creating a two-way exchange where information and experiences are shared, and feedback is received and respected. This reciprocal engagement is critical to deepening trust and understanding in any relationship.

The chapter illustrates that sharing knowledge and positivity goes beyond mere information dissemination. It's about building trust through consistent, helpful, and optimistic interactions. Individuals can significantly enhance their trustworthiness by being a source of knowledge and a beacon of positivity, contributing to more robust, more cohesive personal and professional networks.

Influence of Cultural Background on Trust

This part provides insightful perspectives on how trust is perceived and established differently across cultures. The example of transitioning from Cameroon to America vividly illustrates the challenges and opportunities in trust-building across different cultural contexts.

Cultural background plays a significant role in shaping how trust is formed and maintained. Different cultures have unique values, norms, and expectations that influence their understanding and expression of trust. For instance, some cultures may build trust gradually, emphasizing long-term relationships and proven reliability. In others, trust might be given more readily, with a focus on immediate rapport and connection.

The chapter illustrates this with the transition from Cameroon to America. In Cameroon, trust might be deeply intertwined with community relationships, where trust is fostered within known networks and through established social bonds.

Moving to America, the basis of trust might shift to more individualistic criteria, such as personal integrity, professionalism, and consistency in actions. This shift requires adapting to new ways of establishing credibility and reliability.

Understanding these cultural nuances is crucial for effective communication and relationship-building in diverse settings. It involves recognizing and respecting different approaches to trust and finding ways to bridge cultural gaps.

For example, someone used to a culture where trust is implicit in community relationships might need to focus more on explicit communication and demonstration of reliability in a culture where trust is not assumed.

Moreover, the chapter discusses the importance of cultural sensitivity in building trust. Being aware of and respectful of different cultural expectations and norms is critical to forming genuine connections. This sensitivity can manifest in various forms, from adapting communication styles to understanding different attitudes towards commitments and time management.

In essence, the chapter on the influence of cultural background on trust highlights that trust is not a one-size-fits-all concept. It varies widely across cultural landscapes and successfully navigating these differences is vital for building and sustaining trust in an increasingly interconnected world.

This understanding enriches the broader lessons of the chapter, which collectively underscore the multifaceted nature of trust as an essential component of personal, professional, and communal life.

CHAPTER SEVEN

ACCEPTING CHANGE

"Change is inevitable; growth is optional."

—John C. Maxwell

"ACCEPTING CHANGE" IS like upgrading your mindset from the old-school flip phone to the latest smartphone. It means being open and relaxed with the idea that stuff around us can and will change. It's like realizing that your favorite ice cream flavor may not always be chocolate chip, and that's okay.

Accepting Change may begin with uncertainty and hesitation, but you'll experience a thrilling and transformative adventure once you buckle up and embrace it. It's about letting go of the fear of the unknown and welcoming new possibilities with open arms.

The benefits lead to personal growth, adaptability, and resilience. You become the kind of person who can dance through the ever-changing rhythms of life.

Accepting Change opens doors to new opportunities, relationships, and experiences. It bothers me that you didn't think it was possible. It's like discovering a hidden treasure chest of adventures. Plus, it keeps life from getting boring! "Accepting Change" is not just a concept - it's your ticket to a more exciting, vibrant, and flexible life. Embrace it, and you'll see how Change becomes your trusty sidekick on life's flight. Get ready to unlock your full potential because the sky is the limit when we work together and accept Change!

Accepting Career Changes

Accepting career change has an incredible impact when we work together. To us, it all began way back in high school when we had a dream to become a medical doctor. Little did we know that life had a different plan for us!

My parents (Charles) couldn't afford medical school, but I wasn't about to let that stop me from pursuing my dreams. I had the opportunity to take an entrance exam for the Advanced Teachers Training College in Cameroon. Most of my peers were diving into the same profession through bribery and corruption. However, fortune favored me that year. I didn't pay a bribe to anyone, and I passed the exam, landing a spot in the school of education.

There I was, shifting gears from my initial dream of becoming a doctor to a path in teaching. It was quite the transition, but I was determined to keep moving forward. Then, destiny led me to the United States, where I thought I would continue my career in teaching. Little did I know that the American system had twists, and I had to adapt.

Nursing became my new calling, a job I had yet to plan for initially. But through all these twists and turns, one thing remained constant: my unwavering determination to concentrate and keep moving forward. Life has a funny way of throwing curveballs at us, and we need to be flexible and embrace Change when it comes knocking.

Then, we had this conversation that would change our lives and help us significantly impact our community—stumbling upon a job posting that led to a discussion about the importance of financial planning and having policies in place for our family's future.

We asked ourselves, "What if something was to happen to us? Where would our children go? What would become of them?"

These are questions for everyone to personalize and act for yourself or tell others because as we pray for good health, we should prepare for life's uncertainties. These questions led us to explore the world of financial planning.

We realized that this wasn't just a business but a means to help others secure their legacy and financial future. It was about providing peace of mind and ensuring that we could be taken care of in times of sickness and that our loved ones would be cared for even in our absence. With this newfound perspective, we dove into financial planning, knowing that it was more than just a job; it was a way to make a real difference in people's lives.

Life as a financial professional has been rewarding in more ways than one. It's not only about the money, although that's certainly a perk. It's about the fulfillment of helping families protect their future and, at the same time, ensuring our financial stability. Compared to my nursing job, the reduced stress has been a breath of fresh air. We can concentrate on our work, educate people on financial planning essentials, and still have time for our family.

We dabbled in and out of educating ourselves on finances. Still, in 2021, we decided the only way to make our money work for us was to dedicate time to pursuing financial knowledge. We had become more informed and educated about the business, and our perspective has evolved.

If someone were to ask us for advice on pursuing a similar career, we would tell them this: Hard work and commitment are your best friends. With dedication and a strong work ethic, you will succeed. Persistence is also crucial, especially in this field. It would be best to keep pushing forward, even when things get tough. But more than anything, it helps you see the importance of financial planning. It's not just about the money; it's about securing the lives of your loved ones, both in your presence and their absence. Make them realize that what you do is not just a job; it's a way to provide peace of mind and build a lasting legacy.

My (Charles's) trip from wanting to be a medical doctor to becoming a financial professional has been entirely of Change and adaptation. It has taught me the importance of flexibility, hard work, and the power of making a difference in people's lives.

So, let's all work together, embrace Change, and positively impact our communities. When we work together, Change is possible and incredibly rewarding.

Accepting Challenges

If you're considering jumping into this exciting and rewarding career path of financial planning, first acknowledge that it's not just about making money for yourself; it's about securing your future and caring for your loved ones. Let's dive into why you should consider becoming a financial professional and how to get started on this fantastic journey.

Imagine you've been in this country for a while, working hard, earning your keep, and enjoying life to the fullest. It's all going great until one day, life throws you uncertainty. You fall sick, or worse, you can no longer work.

The big question is, what's in your savings account? What's your backup plan? If you're drawing a blank, don't sweat it; you're not alone. We've all been there, living for today and not thinking much about tomorrow. But here's the fact– tomorrow might arrive sooner than expected. If you're a family person, you've got an even bigger reason to consider this career. Imagine your kids, your spouse, or your loved ones. What happens to them if you're sick or not around anymore? Do you want them to struggle, or do you want to leave them with the resources to thrive and succeed? Here is where being a financial professional comes into play.

When we started down this path, we faced plenty of skeptics. People would say, "You're new here. What do you know?" Or, "They just want to discourage you."

But we didn't let their doubts get to me. We had something that gave us the ultimate confidence booster – a license. The government doesn't just hand out rights to anyone who asks for one. It's a stamp of approval that says, "Hey, you're legit, and you're here to help people, not to scam them." When Mr. Gilbert Fon showed us his license, we said, "Okay, this is the real deal." It hit us that this isn't just a side gig or some get-rich-quick scheme; it's a serious business. The license gives you credibility and is your golden ticket to offering valuable financial advice and solutions.

If you're considering becoming a financial professional, assess your situation first. How long have you been in this country, and what's in your account? If life shows you the back, will you have something to fall back on? It's all about securing your future first. And trust us, you want to avoid being in a position where you wish you'd started planning earlier or, better still, be in a position of saying, "Had I known?". So, start now. It's always possible to take control of your financial destiny. Harvest your prosperity by getting what(policy) you think is of value to you and your loved ones.

Next, think about your family. What legacy do you want to leave if you have kids or loved ones? Do you want them to work for someone else for the rest of their lives, or do you want to empower them to become employers themselves? The answer is straightforward. You want the best for them, and that's where your role as a financial professional comes into play.

Here's what we love about this career: it's all about helping people. You get to be a superhero, not with a cap, but with financial knowledge and expertise. You're not just crunching numbers; you're changing lives. You're helping people secure their futures, achieve their dreams, and protect their families.

The first step to getting started is to get educated. You don't have to be a financial genius from the get-go. You'll learn as you go, and that's all part of the fun. Look for courses and programs to help you gain the knowledge and skills you need to become a financial professional. Trust us, it's worth the investment in you. Networking is also a vital component of this journey. Connect with experienced professionals in the field, attend seminars, and join industry events. You are learning from those who have been there and done that is invaluable. You'll pick up tips, tricks, and insights that you won't find in any textbook. And remember the license - It's your ticket to the big leagues. You'll need to meet the requirements your local government or relevant financial authorities set to obtain one. This ensures you're up to the task and committed to ethical financial practices.

For the rewards: Being a financial professional isn't just about making money (though that's a nice perk). It's about the satisfaction of helping others achieve their financial goals. It's about securing your future and your family's future. It's about becoming a trusted advisor in your community. You'll also have the flexibility to build your own business. You can set your hours, choose your clients, and design your services to meet their needs. This isn't a one-size-fits-all career; it's a journey you can shape to fit your aspirations because no pyramid scheme overtakes it. Overtaking is not forbidden but is allowed.

In finance, there's always room for growth and advancement. You can specialize in areas that resonate with you, whether retirement planning, investment strategies, or life insurance. The opportunities are endless, and you can keep expanding your knowledge and skills to stay at the top of your game. Finally, it's essential to keep the fire alive. Stay motivated and passionate about what you do. Remember the bigger picture: you're making a difference in people's lives. You're not just pushing numbers; you're shaping futures.

Becoming a financial professional is a journey of self-improvement, knowledge, and service. It's a path to financial security for yourself and ensuring your family is cared for. It's a chance to become a hero in your community, a trusted advisor, and a catalyst for Change. So, what are you waiting for? Take that first step and embark on this incredible journey of helping others while securing your financial future. It's a win-win, and we promise you won't regret It.

Takeaways from Accepting Change
Embracing the Unpredictable
The essence of this lesson lies in understanding and valuing the unexpected changes life presents us. Gillian and Charles, each with their distinct career aspirations, found their paths taking unexpected turns, leading them to new, uncharted territories. This narrative illustrates that life's journey is rarely a straight path but a winding road filled with surprises and opportunities.

Embracing the unpredictable is about dealing with change and actively welcoming it. It's about recognizing that unforeseen changes can open doors to previously unimaginable possibilities. For Gillian and Charles, although initially challenging, each twist and turn in their journey eventually led to personal growth and fulfillment. This aspect of their story is a powerful reminder that the most significant opportunities often arise from unexpected places.

It also highlights the importance of adaptability and flexibility for navigating uncertainty. Gillian and Charles' ability to adapt to new situations, to reassess and realign their goals and aspirations, showcases the value of being open to change. This adaptability enabled them to transform potential setbacks into stepping stones toward success.

In "Embracing the Unpredictable," you are encouraged to view change not as an obstacle but as an integral part of life's adventure. We open ourselves to possibilities when we accept and adapt to change. It teaches us that while we may not always have control over the changes in our lives, we control how we respond to them. By embracing change with a positive mindset and a willingness to grow, we can turn the unpredictability of life into a source of strength and enrichment.

Resilience in Career Transitions

Gillian and Charles' story vividly illustrates resilience in the face of career transitions. Their shift from initial professions in teaching and nursing to the world of financial planning epitomizes the courage and adaptability required to navigate significant career changes. This chapter emphasizes that such transitions, while often daunting, can be the catalysts for discovering new passions and unlocking potential that may have lain dormant.

Their journey underscores the notion that a career need not be a linear path but can be a dynamic journey of exploration and growth. Gillian and Charles encountered various challenges as they left their established careers. However, their determination to succeed and willingness to learn new skills in financial planning demonstrates that with resilience, one can adapt to change and thrive in new environments.

For Gillian and Charles, delving into financial planning was not just a professional shift but a journey toward aligning their work with their evolving personal goals and aspirations. It teaches the valuable lesson that our careers can and should evolve as we do, reflecting our current passions, interests, and life situations.

Moreover, their story inspires those hesitant to make a career change, highlighting that pursuing a different path is never too late. This lesson is particularly pertinent in today's fast-changing world, where new and existing industries evolve rapidly. It encourages readers to remain open to new possibilities and to view change not as a threat but as an opportunity for growth and fulfillment.

The Importance of Financial Education

In the narrative of Gillian and Charles, the move towards financial planning is more than a career transition; it symbolizes the pivotal role of financial literacy in shaping one's future. Their journey into financial planning underlines the profound impact of a solid understanding of finances on personal security and prosperity. This chapter highlights their journey and spotlights the universal necessity of financial education.

Their experiences reveal that financial literacy is not a luxury but a fundamental necessity for everyone, transcending career choices and socioeconomic backgrounds. By gaining insight into financial planning, Gillian and Charles could make informed decisions that secured their future and provided a safety net for their family. This aspect of their story underscores that being financially educated equips individuals with the tools to build a more stable and prosperous life.

This lesson delves deeper into the various facets of financial education, from budgeting and saving to investing and planning for retirement. It illustrates that managing money effectively is crucial in today's ever-changing economic landscape. It's about more than just accumulating wealth; it's about making informed decisions that ensure long-term financial well-being.

Furthermore, financial literacy should be an ongoing pursuit. As Gillian and Charles' story shows, the world of finance is constantly evolving, and staying informed is critical to navigating it successfully. They exemplify that being financially literate is empowering, giving individuals the confidence to control their financial destiny.

Learning to Adapt and Grow

This powerfully showcases how life's inevitable changes, particularly in the realm of careers, can be embraced as vital opportunities for learning, growth, and self-improvement. Gillian and Charles' journey is a prime example of this adaptive growth mindset. Their transition into new professional spheres and acquiring new skills underscore the enriching potential of embracing change, even when it appears intimidating or challenging at first glance.

The narrative of Gillian and Charles is replete with instances where they had to step out of their comfort zones and venture into uncharted territories. This required a change in their professional roles and a significant shift in their mindset. They demonstrate that adapting to change is more than a survival tactic; it is an active personal and professional advancement strategy. Each new challenge they faced became an avenue for acquiring new knowledge and skills, enriching their overall life experience.

Building a Legacy Through Change

This section in "Accepting Change" eloquently illustrates the profound impact of creating a lasting legacy through the willingness to embrace life's shifts. Gillian and Charles' transition into financial planning is portrayed as a pursuit of personal achievement and a journey toward establishing a legacy that extends beyond themselves. Their story exemplifies the notion that embracing change is not just about adapting to new circumstances; it's about seizing these moments as opportunities to positively influence and contribute to their family's and broader community's well-being.

Building a legacy involves a forward-looking vision that considers the long-term impact of one's actions. For Gillian and Charles, the decision to enter financial planning was driven by a desire to ensure financial security and prosperity, not just for themselves, their children, and the people around them. Their move symbolizes a shift from focusing solely on individual success to fostering a communal sense of security and stability.

Moreover, this lesson underscores how embracing change and adapting to new roles can positively contribute to society. Through their work in financial planning, Gillian and Charles have educated and empowered others in their community to make informed financial decisions. This aspect of their journey highlights the potential to create a ripple effect of positive change that transcends generations.

In addition, their story serves as an inspiring reminder that a meaningful legacy is often built on the foundation of continuous learning, adaptability, and a commitment to serve others. By leveraging their skills and knowledge in financial planning, they have established a legacy beyond financial wealth; it encompasses enriching lives through education and empowerment.

CHAPTER EIGHT

THE POWER OF FINANCIAL LITERACY

"Never stand begging for that which you have the power to earn."

—Miguel de Cervantes

FINANCIAL LITERACY IS like the magic stick of the money world. It's all about understanding the ABCs of finances, from budgeting, saving, investing, and managing debt. Life has its ups and downs. One moment, you're on top of the world, and the next, you're navigating a financial storm. To make the most of it, you've got to be financially literate.

Financial literacy helps you understand how you can build cash value over time. You must make those cash values grow and use them to secure your future; you must know how to manage your policy wisely. You need to understand how to allocate your funds within the procedure, how to strategize for tax benefits, and when to take withdrawals or loans without jeopardizing your financial future. Financial literacy is your compass in this exciting voyage.

Master your finances and watch your future take off like a rocket because of the compounding effect. It's your life, money, and adventure, so why not make it thrilling?

Building a Secure Future

We used to think talking about finance was as fun as watching paint dry, but once we discovered the magic of it, my perspective did a 180! So, what does it mean to "Build a Secure Future"? It's all about creating a financial safety net that lets you relax, knowing your family's future is in good hands. It's that feeling of confidently walking through life's twists and turns, knowing you have a rock-solid plan.

1. Tax Benefits That Make You Smile

With the right insurance and investments, your cash value grows tax-deferred with no taxes on the growth, and you can even access the money tax-free when you do it right. Now, that's music to our ears! Imagine your money quietly working for you, and you don't have to share a slice of your hard-earned dough with the taxman. That's more money for your future dreams and aspirations, whether sending your kids to college, traveling the world, or retiring in style.

2. Flexible Premiums for Real Life

Life doesn't always follow a straight path. Many policies let you adjust your premiums within certain limits. If your budget is tight for a month, dial it down. And when you're feeling flush, you can increase your contributions. It's like a financial superhero suit that adapts to your needs.

3. Cash Value Growth That Beats the Piggy Bank

Sure, you could toss your spare change into a piggy bank and hope it grows, but Index Universal Life (IUL) insurance takes your cash to the next level. Your money is tied to the stock market index performance with suitable investments. Your cash value grows when the market is doing well, and your principal is protected when it's not.

4. Loan Options: Your Money, Your Rules

There are times when you need some extra cash. The suitable investments allow you to take out policy loans against your cash value. This isn't the same as raiding your savings account; it's borrowing against your insurance policy. The best part is that you set the terms. You can pay it back on your schedule without penalties.

5. Death Benefit: A Gift for Your Loved Ones

While discussing the future, remember the importance of leaving a financial legacy for your beloveds. You want your beneficiaries to receive a death benefit if the unexpected happens. It's wrapping a financial safety net around your family, ensuring they're taken care of when you're no longer around.

6. Living Benefits: Protecting Your Lifestyle

Some policies offer living benefits, which give you access to a portion of your death benefit. At the same time, you're still alive if you're diagnosed with a terminal illness or have other qualifying medical conditions. It's an extra layer of protection for your health and well-being, which will not frustrate you and your family in case you fall sick of either chronic, critical, or terminal illness (the number one cause of bankruptcy).

7. Peace of Mind: The Real Deal

Building a secure future is about more than just numbers and investments. It's about that warm and fuzzy feeling when you know you have a plan and are prepared for whatever life throws.

The more knowledge you have, the more you can use it as a financial GPS that keeps you on the right path, even when the road gets bumpy. With the tax advantages, flexibility, cash value growth, loan options, death benefits, and living benefits that good policies bring, we feel we've got the tools to face the future with a grin. The policy you can afford becomes the prosperity you will harvest.

If you've ever dreamed of a secure future with more money in your pocket, greater flexibility in your financial decisions, and the peace of mind that comes with it, it might be time to explore the world of finances. It's your ticket to a brighter tomorrow, and who doesn't want that? Cheers to building a secure future and living life to the fullest!

Leaving a Legacy

Leaving a legacy is not just a concept for the rich and famous; we can aim for it. And what better way to explore this idea than through the wise words of someone who's been there and done that?

Imagine you're sitting in a room with a cup of coffee, and an experienced financial professional leans in, eyes twinkling with wisdom, and says, "What I would like to tell somebody to join this or to be a financial professional is one thing - you are not only helping yourself."

Doesn't that statement grab your attention? Let's break it down!

Legacy Building Starts with You

Our financial drive often begins with taking care of number one, and that's perfectly fine. The first part of the quote urges us to consider our well-being. How long have you been in this country? What do you have in your account? These questions make you ponder your financial security. If you happen to fall sick, what's your safety net? These are essential questions to ask yourself.

The Unpredictability of Life

Life is full of surprises, and not all of them are pleasant. The quote reminds us that none of us knows when we might be unable to work. The question is, "What have you kept in your account?" In other words, do you have a financial cushion to fall back on during those tough times? This isn't about being a pessimist; it's about being prepared. Being sick can only be a matter of when and not if.

Planning for a Life You Love

If you plan to enjoy life to the fullest, right up to the day you go to your grave, it's time to learn. Learning about finances and planning for your future is about something other than damaging your fun. It's about securing a lot that's as exciting as your present. So, what's your game plan?

Start Planning Now

The most potent part of the quote is the reminder that tomorrow might be too late. Time flies, and you face life's challenges without a financial safety net before you know it. So, what are you waiting for? The sooner you start planning, the brighter your financial future will be.

Your Family's Future

Now, let's shift our focus from ourselves to our loved ones. The financial world isn't just about personal wealth; it's also about securing your family's future. If you're in love with the kids and family God has blessed you with, the question arises: what have you set aside for them?

Think about it. Do you want your loved ones to work for someone else for their entire lives, or do you dream of them employing others and building their legacy? Your financial decisions can make a significant impact on their future.

Our Personal Experiences

Reflecting on our lives, we can't help but be thankful for the opportunities my parents created for us. They worked tirelessly to send us to school and set us on a better future. Their efforts have been a constant source of inspiration for us.

If we're blessed with our kids, we want to do more than send them to school. We want to give them the tools and opportunities to secure their future and help others. It's about paying it forward and leaving a legacy of empowerment. Giving them financial education, which will never be taught in school, is an added advantage because they will join the crusade at the minimum required age.

An Open Check for Your Legacy

Leaving a legacy compares the opportunity to join the financial world to being handed an "open check." Imagine that! You get to decide how much you want to write on that check. It's like a blank canvas where you can paint the picture of your financial legacy. The financial world isn't about limiting your dreams but amplifying them. You're shaping not only your future but your family's future, and even extend your influence to help others achieve their dreams. The possibilities are endless.

Please boldly say - leaving a legacy isn't just for the elites. It's a flight that starts with caring for yourself, planning for the unexpected, and envisioning a life you love. It's about ensuring your family's well-being and empowering them to create their legacy. As you ponder these ideas, remember that the financial world is where you can craft your destiny.

Start building your legacy now because, in the end, it's not about how much you have; it's about what you do with what you have. So, if you're looking for an opportunity that allows you to shape your financial future and make a lasting impact, take a page from the wise words we've explored today. Your legacy awaits – it's time to write your story!

Takeaways from the Power of Financial Literacy

Understanding the Basics Leads to Empowerment

This establishes that financial literacy is the cornerstone of personal empowerment. It highlights how a fundamental understanding of core financial concepts like budgeting, saving, investing, and managing debt is instrumental in taking control of one's financial future. Gillian and Charles' journey exemplifies how mastering these basics can transform an individual's relationship with money, turning it from a source of anxiety and uncertainty into one of strength and opportunity.

The metaphor of a 'magic stick' vividly illustrates that financial literacy is akin to having a powerful tool at one's disposal. It's not merely about keeping track of expenses or saving a portion of income.

Instead, it's about strategically leveraging financial knowledge to build a foundation of stability and growth. This approach to managing finances allows individuals to confidently steer through the complexities of the financial world, making informed decisions that align with their long-term goals and aspirations.

Moreover, this serves as a clarion call for readers to view financial education as a necessity and an avenue for empowerment. It emphasizes that being financially literate equips people with the skills and confidence required to navigate the ebbs and flows of economic life effectively. It transforms the way individuals perceive and interact with money, fostering a sense of control and competency. By embracing financial education, readers can unlock their potential to create a future that is not only financially secure but also prosperous and fulfilling.

Financial Planning for Long-Term Growth

This lesson underscores the importance of incrementally building cash value over time, not as a mere savings exercise, but as a strategic, deliberate action towards achieving financial prosperity. The narrative elucidates how wise financial planning and astute policy management are crucial, emphasizing the need for a well-rounded understanding of effectively allocating funds.

It further explores the tactical aspects of financial planning, such as leveraging tax benefits to maximize financial gains. It offers insights into the intricacies of navigating the tax implications of various financial decisions, highlighting how adept planning can significantly enhance one's financial position. Additionally, the discussion extends to making prudent choices regarding withdrawals and loans, ensuring these actions align with long-term financial objectives and not inadvertently undermine one's financial security.

Moreover, this part of the book illustrates that a comprehensive approach to financial literacy is more than understanding basic financial concepts; it's about understanding financial products and market dynamics. This more profound knowledge enables individuals to make informed decisions that harness the power of their finances, leading to substantial growth over time. The chapter aims to equip readers with the tools and insights necessary to build a robust financial foundation that not only withstands the test of time but also paves the way for a future marked by financial security and prosperity.

In essence, "Financial Planning for Long-Term Growth" is a vital lesson in managing finances with foresight and sophistication. It encourages readers to see financial planning as an integral part of their journey toward financial independence, emphasizing that long-term financial growth and security are within reach with the proper knowledge and strategies.

Compounding Effect and Financial Future

The concept of the compounding effect in finance forms a pivotal part of this chapter, illuminating the transformative power of this principle in shaping one's financial future. The chapter elucidates that when individuals master managing their finances, they unlock the potential for exponential growth in their financial resources. This compounding effect, often referred to as the 'eighth wonder of the world,' demonstrates how the reinvestment of earnings can lead to wealth accumulating at an accelerating rate over time.

This section is a compelling motivator for readers to shift their focus from the allure of immediate financial gratification to a long-term vision of wealth accumulation. It emphasizes that consistency in financial strategies—such as regular investments and reinvesting returns—can significantly amplify one's financial assets. This process is akin to a snowball effect, where initial modest gains gather momentum and size, culminating in a substantial sum over the years.

In summary, "Compounding Effect and Financial Future" imparts a crucial financial lesson: small, consistent, and intelligent financial decisions can lead to substantial growth over time. This insight is vital for anyone looking to secure their financial future and underscores the importance of patience, discipline, and strategic planning in personal finance. By embracing the compounding effect, readers are equipped with a powerful tool to grow their wealth and transform their financial future into a successful and exhilarating journey.

Building a Secure Financial Safety Net

This chapter strongly emphasizes the critical need for a financial safety net as a fundamental component of a secure future. It delves into how meticulous financial planning and prudent insurance choices can be a bulwark against unpredictable events, offering much-needed peace of mind. The narrative goes beyond mere wealth accumulation; it's about constructing a robust buffer that safeguards the individual and their family from potential financial upheavals.

The discussion in this chapter revolves around the concept that financial security entails more than having a substantial amount of money in the bank. It's about strategically positioning oneself and one's family to withstand financial storms that may arise. This involves a comprehensive approach, encompassing savings, investments, insurance, and emergency funds, all meticulously orchestrated to create a resilient financial fortress.

Additionally, the chapter underscores the importance of insurance as a pivotal tool in this safety net. It illustrates how the right insurance policies can act as a lifeline in adverse situations, whether dealing with unexpected medical expenses, loss of income, or even the financial ramifications of death. These policies can provide a financial cushion, ensuring that life's uncertainties do not translate into catastrophic financial setbacks.

Moreover, this lesson about building a financial safety net is presented as a prudent financial strategy and a responsible act towards oneself and one's loved ones. It's about taking proactive steps today to secure a stable, worry-free future. The chapter encourages readers to view financial planning as an act of care and foresight, reminding them that today's decisions can profoundly impact their and their family's future.

Leaving a Lasting Legacy

This chapter illuminates the profound and enduring impact of legacy building through astute financial planning. It advocates that financial literacy and effective planning go beyond personal gain, extending into family and community enrichment. The concept of legacy in this context transcends the accumulation of wealth; it's about forging a path others can follow, providing a template for financial stability and success that can benefit future generations.

The narrative conveys that today's financial decisions are not just about immediate gratification or individual success. Instead, they are building blocks for a legacy that will stand the test of time. This chapter emphasizes that a well-thought-out financial plan has the potential to influence positively and shape the lives of one's children, grandchildren, and even the community at large. It's about creating opportunities, opening doors, and setting up the next generation for success.

Furthermore, the chapter encourages readers to view financial planning as a tool for impactful legacy building. It's about instilling values such as financial responsibility, the importance of saving and investing, and the power of giving back. When passed down, these principles become more than just financial strategies; they transform into life lessons that guide and support future generations.

Moreover, this lesson on legacy building is a call to action for readers to take a proactive approach to crafting their financial narratives. It inspires them to think about the mark they want to leave on the world, how they wish to be remembered, and how their financial planning can contribute to a legacy of prosperity, wisdom, and generosity.

CHAPTER NINE

HELPING COMMUNITIES

"As you grow older, you will discover that you have two hands: One for helping yourself, the other for helping others."

—Audrey Hepburn

"IF YOU SEE SOMETHING good, share it with somebody else."

This is a simple yet powerful idea, and it's something that we genuinely believe in. Helping the community means reaching out and positively impacting the people around you. It's about coming together to support, empower, and uplift each other. It's about sharing knowledge, resources, and opportunities rather than hoarding them for ourselves.

The experience of moving from Africa, specifically Cameroon, to America and noticing that some people don't always encourage others or share the good things they come across. Instead, they quickly say, "You can't do it."

The sentiment is common, especially when pursuing our dreams and goals. Have you ever had a moment when you were excited about a new project, an idea, or a career path, and someone just shot it down with a "You can't do it"? It's like a bucket of cold water thrown on your fiery enthusiasm. But the truth is, you CAN do it, and often, those naysayers project their fears and insecurities onto you.

But despite the discouragement and skepticism, we were confident we could achieve our goals. A little voice whispered, "You've got this!" And guess what? It was right! As we went through the struggles and acquired the skills we needed, we reached our goals, and that has been a powerful testament to the human spirit and determination.

For us, we didn't stop at achieving our dreams. Instead, we realized that we could use our success to impact others. And that's a crucial part of helping communities. When you make it, you don't just take it and run. No, you turn back and extend a hand to pull others up. It's like a chain reaction of positivity and progress.

How to Do It

To help the community, you need to take small steps, one day at a time. So, how can we do it?

Share Knowledge

Knowledge is power, and sharing it is a powerful way to help others. If you have expertise in a particular field, mentor someone just starting. Offer advice, guidance, and encouragement. You can even start a blog or a YouTube channel to share your knowledge with a broader audience.

Support Local Businesses

Local businesses are the backbone of communities. When you buy from them, you're not just getting a product or service but helping someone's dream thrive. Our advice: shop local, dine local, and recommend local businesses to your friends and family.

Volunteer

Giving your time and skills to a cause you care about is a fantastic way to help your community. Whether volunteering at a food bank, a shelter, or a local school, your efforts can make a significant difference.

Be Inclusive

Embrace diversity and inclusion. Don't judge people based on their background, race, or gender. Encourage everyone to sit at the table and be part of the conversation. An inclusive community is a thriving community.

Share Positive Stories

Remember the quote we mentioned earlier? "If you see something good, share it with somebody else." It's as simple as that. Share positive stories, achievements, and opportunities with your community. Let them know there's good stuff out there for those who qualify to join the crusade of no family left behind.

Create a Safe Space

Sometimes, all people need is a safe space to share their thoughts, concerns, and ideas. Be that safe space. Listen, empathize, and offer your support when needed.

Organize Community Events

Bring your community together by organizing events and gatherings. Whether it's a neighborhood clean-up, a street party, or a charity run, events foster a sense of togetherness and strengthen community bonds.

Mentorship

If you've been fortunate in your career or personal life, consider becoming a mentor. Whether it's helping someone with career advice, academic guidance, or personal development, your experience can be a guiding light for someone else, just like our own story, which is our turning point.

Be a Role Model

Lead by example. Show your community what it means to be compassionate, responsible, and proactive. Your actions can act as an inspiration for others to follow suit.

Helping communities isn't just about giving; it's about receiving, too. When we help others, we experience a multitude of personal benefits:

A profound sense of satisfaction comes from knowing you've positively impacted someone's life. It's that warm and fuzzy feeling that money can't buy. By actively participating in your community, you build stronger connections with your neighbors, colleagues, and friends. These connections can provide support when you need it and enrich your life in countless ways.

Helping communities often involves stepping out of your comfort zone. You learn new skills, gain new perspectives, and become a better person. As more individuals get involved in helping their communities, the community as a whole becomes more robust and more resilient. This benefits everyone living within it.

You can catalyze positive change by sharing knowledge and opportunities. You might help someone start a small business, find their passion, or achieve a dream they thought was out of reach. Being known as someone who actively contributes to their community can improve your personal and professional reputation. People are more likely to trust and collaborate with individuals committed to the betterment of their community.

When you help someone, they're more likely to help others, creating a beautiful ripple effect. It's like planting seeds of kindness that grow into a forest of goodwill. Please stand up, friends, and let's commit to helping our communities. Let's be the ones who say, "You CAN do it!" Let's be the ones who share the good stuff and uplift those around us. Remember, it's not about how much you can do; it's about doing what you can. Every small effort counts:

together, we can create a world of positive change, one community at a time.

In the words of the wise person from Cameroon, " "If I see anything good I like to share it with others. Those who will listen and pay attention to it will have their answer. Always try to be good or share good things; don't keep it to yourself." It's a philosophy we can all live by – sharing the good stuff for a better world.

Creating a Ripple Effect

You might have heard this term tossed around - creating a ripple effect, but what does it mean? Picture this: You throw a pebble into a calm, glassy lake. As it makes contact, a series of ever-expanding ripples emanate from the point of impact, reaching far and wide. That is the ripple effect in a nutshell.

In our everyday lives, the ripple effect is about the positive influence we can have on the world through our actions, words, and choices. It's about starting a chain reaction of goodness and inspiring others to do the same. By doing something good, you create a ripple that touches lives, motivates others, and changes the world bit by bit. It's like a domino effect but with love and kindness!

You might wonder, "How can I be part of this great move?" we've got a boatload of ideas on how you can become a ripple-maker extraordinaire.

Be the Change You Wish to See

Gandhi said it best: "Be the change you wish to see in the world." Want a kinder, more compassionate world? Start by being kind and forgiving yourself. Set an example by treating others how you'd like to be treated.

Small Acts, Big Impact

Remember, you don't need to move mountains to make waves; even tiny pebbles can create ripples. Smile at a stranger, hold the door open, or offer a helping hand. Kindness can brighten someone's day and set the ripple effect in motion.

Volunteer Your Time and Skills

Another fantastic way to create ripples of positivity is through volunteering. Whether helping at a local shelter, tutoring a student, or participating in community clean-up events, your time and skills can make a big difference.

Spread Positivity Online

In the age of social media, your online presence matters, too. Use your platforms to share inspirational stories and words of encouragement. Your positivity can resonate with others and encourage them to do the same.

Support Charities and Causes

Find a cause you're passionate about and support it. Whether donating to a charity, fundraising for a local organization or simply spreading awareness, your involvement can create a ripple of change for a cause close to your heart.

Share Knowledge

Education is one of the most potent catalysts for change. Share your knowledge, skills, and expertise with those eager to learn because sharing develops expertise. It could be as simple as mentoring a young professional or teaching someone a new skill.

Be an Active Listener

Sometimes, all it takes to create a ripple of change is to lend a sympathetic ear. Be an active listener for friends, family, and even strangers in need. You might not realize it, but your understanding and support can make a world of difference to someone.

Random Acts of Kindness

Spontaneity can be your greatest ally in creating ripples. Surprise someone with a random act of kindness, like buying a coffee for the person behind you in line or leaving a heartfelt note on a co-worker's desk.

Lead by Example

Suppose you're in a leadership role at work, in your community, or among friends, led by example. Show others how it's done by embodying the values and principles you want to see in those around you.

Create a Ripple Network

Remember, you're not in this alone. Connect with like-minded persons who share your passion for positive change. Together, you can amplify your impact and create waves beyond your wildest dreams.

As you continue creating ripples, there are plenty of personal benefits to being a ripple-maker. First, an undeniable sense of fulfillment and joy comes from knowing you've positively impacted someone's life. The happiness you bring to others will get back to you beautifully. You will be Kind and compassionate when building solid connections with others. You'll be surrounded by people who appreciate your efforts and are more likely to reciprocate your goodwill.

Being part of the ripple effect can boost your well-being. Studies have shown that kindness and selflessness can reduce stress, increase happiness, and improve physical health. Creating ripples encourages personal growth. You'll learn more about yourself, your strengths, and your capacity to impact the world positively. It's a journey of self-discovery and continuous improvement.

Your actions and choices can serve as an inspiration to others. You never know who you might motivate to start their ripple of kindness. By creating a ripple effect, you're leaving a lasting legacy of positivity. Your impact can continue to inspire your generation and those to come.

So, how can you get your ripple groove on and keep the good vibes flowing? It's all about integrating these practices into your daily life and making them a part of who you are.

Consistency is critical, but remember to keep things fun and light-hearted by creating a ripple journal to keep track of your kind acts and the positive reactions they generate. It's like a diary of your ripple adventures. Reflect on your experiences and see how you're making a difference.

You can also set goals for yourself, like "I'll perform one random act of kindness every week." Having specific ambitions will keep you motivated and on track. Go out there and challenge your friends or colleagues to join you on your ripple journey. Compete to see who can create the most ripples in a month. The good books make it clear that blessed is the hand that is given rather than the one that takes. Is that suitable? Testimonies are the smiles that glow from recipients of our charitable acts.

Share your ripple stories with your social circle. You'd be surprised how many people will be inspired to join when they hear about your beautiful work. Or you can connect with other ripple-makers and learn from their experiences. It's a great way to gather new ideas and stay inspired.

There will be days when your ripples seem to go unnoticed, but don't get discouraged. Remember that even the tiniest waves can create significant change, and your efforts make a difference, whether you see it immediately or not.

Infuse playfulness into your ripple-making endeavors. Doing something fun and spontaneous can be the ultimate mood booster for you and those you're helping. You can also celebrate your ripple achievements, whether big or small. Treat yourself to self-care or throw a mini party with friends to commemorate the good vibes you've spread.

Let's create some ripples, my fellow wave-makers! It's an adventure where every action counts, and the more waves we create, the more significant the positive impact we'll have on the world. Remember, you don't need to be a superhero to make a difference. You need a big heart, a positive attitude, and a willingness to throw that pebble of kindness into the world's giant pond.

The ripple effect is a drive of joy, personal growth, and creating a better world, one act of kindness at a time. So, go on, make some waves, and watch the world light up with positivity and love. Together, we can turn those ripples into a tidal wave of change! As I will always say, our communities need us.

Takeaways from Helping Communities

Empowerment Through Sharing Knowledge

The profound impact of sharing knowledge within communities is a central theme in this chapter, vividly illustrated by Gillian's and Charles's experiences. Their journey from humble beginnings to becoming financial educators underscores the transformative power of knowledge sharing. By disseminating vital financial literacy skills, they demonstrate how knowledge can empower individuals. This empowerment goes beyond mere information transfer; it's about equipping people with the tools they need to navigate life's complexities.

Through their narrative, Gillian and Charles reveal how knowledge sharing can catalyze change. Educating others helps individuals make better financial decisions, leading to more robust, secure futures. This process of sharing wisdom does more than inform; it inspires confidence, fosters independence, and encourages self-sufficiency. It's about creating a domino effect where educated individuals can, in turn, educate others, building a community that is robust, informed, and resilient.

Furthermore, this highlights that sharing knowledge is not a one-way street; it's a reciprocal process that enriches both the teacher and the learner. As Gillian and Charles share their expertise, they also learn from the experiences and perspectives of those they teach, leading to a mutual growth process. This knowledge exchange cultivates a sense of community solidarity, where the common goal of collective advancement unites people.

In essence, empowerment through knowledge sharing is a powerful testament to the role of education in community development. It shows that when equipped with the proper knowledge, individuals are better positioned to overcome challenges, seize opportunities, and ultimately drive positive change in their lives and the broader community. This lesson from Gillian and Charles serves as a beacon of hope and a call to action, encouraging us all to share our knowledge and wisdom, thus contributing to the empowerment of our communities.

Encouragement Over Discouragement

Gillian and Charles' story poignantly illustrates the critical role of encouragement in nurturing individual aspirations and strengthening community bonds. Their experiences shed light on the common challenge of skepticism and doubt, especially when pursuing personal dreams and ambitions. However, their journey underscores the transformative power of positive reinforcement over hostile skepticism.

The narrative emphasizes the need for communities to foster an environment where encouragement, rather than discouragement, is the norm. Such an environment enables individuals to confidently pursue their dreams, knowing they have the support and belief of those around them. This encouragement is not just about offering kind words; it's a more profound act of empowering others to believe in their abilities and potential. It's about creating a space where people feel valued and their aspirations are taken seriously.

Moreover, this approach to community building goes beyond individual success. When a community adopts a culture of encouragement, it cultivates a sense of unity and collective strength. It becomes a place where people lift each other, creating a positive cycle of inspiration and achievement. In such communities, when one person succeeds, it sets a precedent and allows others to follow suit.

Gillian and Charles' experiences show that a supportive word or gesture can make a significant difference when faced with doubt. It can be the catalyst that transforms uncertainty into action and dreams into reality. Their story is a call to action for us all to be sources of encouragement in our communities. By uplifting rather than undermining, we contribute to building a supportive network that can withstand challenges and thrive on collective successes. This lesson is an invaluable reminder of the power of encouragement in creating resilient, motivated, and successful communities.

Confidence Against Naysayers

The journey of Gillian and Charles, as depicted in this chapter, powerfully illustrates the importance of maintaining self-confidence in the face of skepticism and negativity. Their story is a compelling testament to the fact that success is achievable, even when surrounded by doubters. This lesson is particularly relevant in a world where naysayers often cloud one's vision and aspirations.

The narrative encourages readers to trust their abilities and potential, emphasizing that self-belief is a crucial ingredient in the recipe for success. It teaches that while external validation is comforting, one's conviction and determination ultimately pave the way to achieving goals. Their experience is a beacon of inspiration, especially to those who encounter skepticism in their personal or professional endeavors.

Furthermore, this lesson highlights the significance of nurturing a strong sense of self-confidence. It's about understanding that while constructive criticism can be beneficial, it's essential to differentiate it from baseless negativity that serves no purpose but to discourage. Gillian and Charles' resilience in the face of doubt exemplifies how confidence can help one overcome obstacles and act as a source of inspiration and strength for others facing similar challenges.

This chapter serves as a potent reminder that while naysayers may be a part of one's journey, they do not define the destination. It underscores the value of believing in oneself, persisting despite challenges, and staying true to one's vision and goals. The story of Gillian and Charles thus becomes a motivating narrative that encourages readers to hold onto their confidence, pursue their dreams with determination, and triumph over the skepticism they may encounter.

Success as a Platform for Impact

The narrative of Gillian and Charles in this chapter eloquently demonstrates how personal success can be leveraged as a powerful tool for community upliftment. Their journey from humble beginnings to achieving significant milestones is a story of individual triumph and an inspiring example of how success can be transformed into a catalyst for broader community impact.

This lesson delves into the ethos of 'giving back,' where success is not seen as an endpoint but as a means to extend support, guidance, and opportunities to others. It underscores the idea that true success transcends personal accolades and wealth – it lies in the ability to use one's achievements as a springboard to foster growth and development within the community.

Gillian and Charles' approach to success demonstrates a profound sense of responsibility and altruism. They embody the principle that the power, perhaps the duty, to impact others positively comes with achievement. This perspective shifts the focus from individualism to communal progress, highlighting how personal achievements can spark a chain reaction of empowerment and success within a community.

Importantly, this lesson also illustrates the concept of mentorship and support. It shows that successful individuals can be pivotal in guiding and inspiring others, particularly those just starting their journey. By sharing their experiences, challenges, and insights, they can help others navigate their paths more effectively.

In essence, the story of Gillian and Charles serves as a poignant reminder that success is most meaningful when it extends beyond personal gains to impact the lives of others. It encourages readers to view their achievements as opportunities to make a difference, create lasting change, and contribute to a cycle of collective success and prosperity within their communities.

Creating a Chain Reaction of Positivity
This encapsulates the transformative power of the 'ripple effect' in community engagement. It paints a vivid picture of how one individual's kindness or generosity can create positive change, thereby significantly impacting the broader community.

The lesson delves into the concept that each person holds the potential to be a catalyst for positive transformation. Simple gestures of goodwill, sharing valuable insights, or helping can have far-reaching consequences, extending well beyond one's immediate environment. This chain reaction is rooted in the idea that positivity begets positivity – a single act of kindness can inspire others, leading to a widespread culture of support, empathy, and collaboration.

By highlighting the importance of initiating positive actions, the chapter encourages readers to recognize their role as change agents in their communities. It suggests that even minor contributions can substantially impact, creating an environment where kindness, support, and positivity flourish.

This concept enriches recipients' and the giver's lives, fostering community, connectedness, and shared purpose. It promotes a sense of collective responsibility where each member contributes to creating a more supportive, understanding, and thriving community.

Overall, this lesson from Gillian and Charles' story is a powerful reminder of the influence of individual actions in shaping the dynamics of a community. It invites readers to embrace the opportunity to be a positive force, understanding that their contributions, no matter how small, can set in motion a wave of beneficial changes that resonate throughout their community.

CHAPTER TEN

CHANGING MINDSETS THROUGH EDUCATION

"Education's purpose is to replace an empty mind with an open one."

—Malcolm Forbes

CHANGING MINDSETS THROUGH education is a quest to uncover a hidden treasure - the treasure of knowledge. With each step you take, you cut through preconceived notions and misconceptions. Education isn't just about textbooks and classrooms; it's about exposing yourself to new ideas, different perspectives, and diverse cultures. It's like opening a window and letting in a gust of fresh air. Suddenly, your world expands, and you realize there's so much more out there.

Have you ever seen a caterpillar transform into a butterfly? Education is like that magical chrysalis, changing your perspective from something limited and crawling to something beautiful and soaring. You learn to appreciate the beauty in diversity, respect different viewpoints, and embrace change.

The power of education lies in its ability to challenge your existing beliefs, encouraging you to question, explore, and adapt. It's like a supercharged upgrade for your mindset, turning it from a clunky old flip phone into a sleek, high-tech smartphone. Education is an ongoing adventure where your mindset is the map, and the possibilities are endless. Get ready to discover the treasure of a more open, accepting, and enlightened world!

How it Would Empower Children

Education is the ultimate superpower for kids, helping them achieve economic independence, make vital decisions, and build that fantastic habit of saving money- it's like giving them the keys to the world!

Economic Independence

As a kid, you have zero knowledge about money – where it comes from, how to make it grow, or how to manage it. That's like playing a video game without instructions – you're doomed to fail! But, when you get educated, it's like leveling up in the game of life. You start learning about different careers, how to set goals, and the skills needed to pursue your dreams.

Education helps you understand that money doesn't just fall from the sky; you must work for it. You learn to invest your time and energy in things, leading to a paycheck to earn money- that magical piece of paper that allows you to buy stuff, go on adventures, and be in charge of your life.

Education also teaches you about financial literacy – a fancy way of saying you learn how to handle money like a pro. You'll know how to budget, save, and make intelligent choices with your hard-earned cash. So, you can splurge a little on things you love and save up for your future. When you're educated, you're more likely to land a job that pays well, which means you can support yourself and maybe even help your family. Economic independence isn't just about making money; it's about being self-reliant and having the confidence to tackle life's challenges head-on.

Enforcing Strong Decision Making

Life is chock-full of choices – big, small, and everything in between. And if you're not equipped with the right tools, it can be like navigating a maze blindfolded. However, education is your trusted map through the maze.

It helps you develop critical thinking skills, like your secret weapons for making intelligent choices. You learn to gather information, weigh pros and cons, and make decisions aligning with your goals and values.

You can spot opportunities a mile away and seize them confidently when educated. You know how to plan your path, set priorities, and stay on track. It's like having a superpower that guides you through the ups and downs of life. When choosing a career without education, you might unthinkingly follow someone else's advice or pick a job that doesn't make you happy. But with education, you can explore your interests, understand your strengths, and choose a career that suits you like a glove. You're not just a passenger in the decision-making process; you're the captain of your ship!

Good decisions often lead to financial success. Choosing a career you're passionate about and skilled in makes you more likely to excel. And when you're great at what you do, people are willing to pay you well for your expertise. Strong decision-making is like a one-way ticket to a bright and prosperous future!

Building the Habit of Saving Mentality

To achieve financial freedom, you must cultivate a habit of saving mentality. Picture your education as the wise sensei in a martial arts movie, teaching you the art of financial discipline. It's like learning to do those fancy Kung Fu moves, but for your money.

Education teaches you the importance of saving money, and it's not just about hoarding cash under your mattress – that's so 20th century! You learn to set financial goals, create a budget, and systematically save money. It's like a savings workout plan but way less sweaty.

You're ready for all life's outcomes when you know how to save. Whether it's a sudden medical bill, a fantastic vacation, or an opportunity to invest, you've got the cash ready to roll. You don't have to rely on others or go into debt; you're financially resilient and prepared for action. Plus, the habit of saving mentality doesn't just apply to emergencies.

It also helps you achieve your long-term dreams, like buying a house, starting a business, or retiring comfortably. The key is that it's not just about saving for a rainy day; it's about securing your sunny days, too!

Education also introduces you to the magical world of investing. You learn how to make your money work for you, so it grows over time through compounding. It's like planting seeds that grow into money trees – and who wouldn't want a money tree, right? Education is like your ticket to economic independence, strong decision-making skills, and the habit of saving mentality. It's like getting the keys to a bright and prosperous future. With education, you're not just a passenger in life's journey; you're the captain of your ship, the master of your financial destiny, and the architect of your dreams.

Soak up knowledge and watch how it transforms your life. It's not just about books and classrooms; it's about empowerment, growth, and becoming the superhero of your own story. Get ready to conquer the world – it's yours for the taking! You choose what you want to generate to represent your generational wealth for you and your family.

Breaking the Cycle of Poverty

There are some valuable life lessons about breaking the cycle of poverty. These lessons come straight from an experience of going through thick and thin but managing to thrive despite the challenges.

Trust in a Higher Power

The main tradition we have at home is we have trust; we trust God first. We always sit and pray together. We believe that God will direct us in all our various activities because we don't do anything by our power." First and foremost, put your trust in a higher power. Believing in something greater than you can provide guidance and strength to overcome obstacles.

Family Bond and Tradition

We have made it clear to our children that they must be like that. And it must maintain that tradition with or without us. Building strong family bonds and preserving traditions can create a supportive foundation for success. Teach your values and ensure they carry them forward.

Hard Work and Commitment

The primary advice I'll give someone is just hard work and commitment. Because if you're not committed to doing something, if you don't put in the hard work in anything or a similar career, you won't succeed. Success is not handed to you; you've got to put in the effort and stay committed to your goals.

Persistence Pays Off

Encourage people and let them see the importance of it, how it will save their lives and even their loved ones, either in their presence or in their absence. It would be best if you stayed persistent in your pursuits, even when others try to discourage you. Persistence often leads to the most rewarding outcomes.

Seek Legitimacy

Some will say no to everything, trying to discourage you. Make sure your endeavors are legitimate. Seek licenses and credentials that boost your credibility and protect you from legal troubles.

Time Management and Purposefulness

One of the skills we were given was being on time and keeping to the deadline. Being purposeful in whatever we must do is taking it seriously and doing it to the best of my ability. Time management and purposefulness are essential. Being punctual and dedicated to your tasks can set you apart from the competition.

Respect Others

Respecting anybody, no matter what they are or how they are. Please show respect to everyone, their status or background notwithstanding. Respect begets respect, and it's a key ingredient in building positive relationships.

Carry Your Attitude Everywhere

The attitude you carry and how you behave in your house, don't think you can go out there and pretend for too long, is usually for a short time. This is because your attitude at home often reflects your true character. Be genuine and carry your values with you wherever you go.

Dress Decently and Respectfully

Learn to dress decently outside... No matter if everybody is accepting it, there is one person that you always have to look up to as a role model.

Dressing decently and respectfully reflects self-worth and respect for others and your values.

Find Mentors

Mentors, especially in this business, are the first to influence us. Our immediate boss is Gilbert Fon, followed by Daniel Fombo. They always encourage us, and they say everybody can make it. Seek out mentors who can guide and inspire you. Their wisdom and encouragement can be invaluable in your journey to success.

Don't Let Discouragement Stop You

Don't mind about discouragement, because people always discourage you. Remember, there will always be naysayers and doubters. Don't let their negativity hold you back. Keep moving forward with determination and perseverance.

We urge you to take the wealth of wisdom from us, persons who know what it takes to break the cycle of poverty. Trust in a higher power, value family traditions, work hard, stay committed, and be persistent.

Seek legitimacy, manage your time wisely, and show respect to others. Carry your attitude and values with you, dress decently, and find mentors who inspire you. And never let discouragement deter you from your path to success.

Life can have challenges, but you can overcome anything with the right mindset and values. Remember, you have the power to shape your destiny, and it all starts with believing in yourself and the values guiding your journey.

Takeaways from Changing Mindsets Through Education

Empowerment Through Community Action

This lesson highlights how individual actions and initiatives can empower entire communities. It showcases that when individuals take proactive steps through volunteering, mentoring, or sharing resources, they can significantly uplift those around them.

This empowerment extends beyond just helping others; it also strengthens the community's fabric, making it more resilient and capable of facing challenges together.

Positive Influence and Role Modeling

Gillian and Charles' journey demonstrates that individuals can inspire others to follow suit by embodying the values of kindness, generosity, and support. This lesson underscores the impact of leading by example and how personal conduct can influence and shape the behaviors and attitudes of others in the community.

Fostering Inclusivity and Diversity

The significance of embracing and promoting inclusivity and diversity within communities. It illustrates how acknowledging and celebrating diverse backgrounds and perspectives can lead to a more cohesive and understanding community environment. This approach enhances social harmony and encourages a richer exchange of ideas and experiences, benefiting the community.

Building Stronger Connections Through Kindness

A key takeaway from this chapter is the power of kindness in building and strengthening community connections. It shows that acts of kindness, big or small, can forge stronger bonds between individuals, fostering a sense of belonging and mutual support. This interconnectedness is crucial for creating a supportive network that members can rely on in need.

Promoting Active Community Engagement

Lastly, the chapter advocates for active engagement and participation in community activities. It highlights that involvement in community events, projects, or initiatives contributes to the community's well-being and provides individuals with purpose and fulfillment. Active engagement encourages a collaborative spirit, where each member plays a vital role in contributing to the community's growth and success.

CHAPTER ELEVEN

EMPOWERING AN ENTREPRENEURIAL SPIRIT

"To any entrepreneur: If you want to do it now. If you don't, you are going to regret it."

—Catherine Cook

EMPOWERING AN ENTREPRENEURIAL spirit is like giving a spark to a blazing fire within. It's about encouraging people to dream big, take risks, and turn their innovative ideas into reality. It's vital because it's the engine that drives innovation, economic growth, and positive change in the world.

These creative minds bring fresh ideas, create job opportunities, and drive economic progress. When you empower an entrepreneurial spirit, you're not just impacting one individual; you're contributing to the growth and prosperity of a community, a nation, and even the world.

Entrepreneurship is vital as the fearless explorers of our age navigate uncharted territory, and they're the reason we have excellent products, services, and solutions that improve our lives. They're the ones who transform problems into opportunities, challenges into victories, and obstacles into stepping stones.

At an early age, I (Gillian) liked to do something. I always wanted money, even though I didn't know what to buy. Even as a child, I had that innate drive to make my dreams a reality. It started with frying ground nuts at the tender age of 10 and eventually led me to cook food and sell it when I was 15. I knew I wanted more from life, and my entrepreneurial spirit thrived.

My journey took an unexpected turn when my dream of becoming a nurse was threatened. I faced financial obstacles that could have shattered my dreams, but I refused to give in and persevered, and when I finally joined the school, I didn't stop there. Completing school was just the beginning, as I discovered that landing a job in my field wasn't guaranteed.

The entrepreneurial fire within me continued to burn bright. I began to explore other avenues to support my family and my dreams. I started a small-scale business selling products like egusi (melon) seeds, peeling and selling them to make ends meet. My resourcefulness was a testament to my unwavering determination.

My journey took me to the United States, but the challenges continued. I noticed a financial trend among my peers—everyone seemed to be talking about car loans and credit cards.

This made me ponder, "If I come on, I have this, and I'm still dependent on a credit card, what will I leave for my children?" It was a pivotal moment of realization for me. I knew I needed to take control of my financial future and leave a legacy for my loved ones.

It was a game-changer for me. Safeguarding my family's future became the driving force behind my decision to delve into the world of financial services.

From that moment on, my transformation was nothing short of remarkable. I eagerly took the plunge into this new endeavor, determined to secure my family's future. I was inspired by the potential financial gains and the peace of mind it offered. Now, I am not just an entrepreneur but also a financial professional, guiding others on the path to financial security and independence. My infectious enthusiasm and dedication to helping others secure their financial future have created a ripple effect.

But what's truly remarkable about my story is my ability to blend my entrepreneurial spirit with a heartfelt desire to help those in need. I have learned a valuable lesson from my father, who once said, "If your money can always sponsor yourself, then you don't have anything. You need to help someone in need. You need to sponsor somebody." And that's precisely what I'm doing.

I realized that my newfound financial journey was not just about personal gain but also about lifting others. My mission goes beyond building a prosperous future for my family; it's about creating a legacy of empowerment and support for future generations. You need to help someone in need. It would be best if you sponsored someone. This philosophy resonates with many, as I champion the idea that true success is not measured solely by personal wealth but by the impact you can make on the lives of others.

Empowering an entrepreneurial spirit is not just about creating successful individuals; it's about nurturing a mindset that can change the world. My journey serves as a testament to the importance of financial independence, not just for oneself but for the well-being of future generations.

You can also turn challenges into opportunities, transform your life, and change the lives of countless others. Empower your entrepreneurial spirit, secure your financial future, and leave a legacy that inspires and uplifts those who follow in your footsteps.

Business is Not About the Dollars in Your Account

Business is not about the dollars in your account but something far more profound, meaningful, and rewarding. The true beauty of running a business lies in a much deeper, more meaningful place. We're not saying money isn't necessary; it is. But it's only a tiny part of the larger picture.

When you embark on your entrepreneurial journey, it's like stepping into a world full of possibilities and uncharted territories. It's not just about making money; it's about making a difference, creating something valuable, and leaving your mark on the world.

Think about it for a moment: What makes a business truly successful? It's not just the dollars piled up in your account; it's your impact on people's lives, the problems you solve, and the value you bring to your customers.

Begin by understanding that businesses exist to solve problems, big or small. Whether providing a better solution for a common issue, making someone's life easier, or addressing a need, your business is there to fill a gap in the market. Also, recognize that companies develop opportunities for the owners and the people they employ, suppliers, and communities. It's a chain reaction that goes beyond the balance sheet.

To succeed in business, you need to be innovative. You must constantly evolve, adapt, and keep up with changing times. This drive for innovation fuels progress and changes the world. It would be best if you built relationships in your business. These connections are invaluable, whether with customers, employees, or fellow entrepreneurs. They create a sense of community and support, often leading to collaborative partnerships that can be game changers.

Running a business is a journey of personal growth. It pushes you to your limits, forces you to learn new things, and helps you adapt to challenges you never thought you could overcome. Your business evolves, and so do you. Business can be about leaving a legacy. It's about your mark on the world, the positive change you bring, and the lasting impact long after you've moved on.

The beauty of entrepreneurship is that it lets you combine your passion and your purpose. It's not just about profit; it's about making a positive impact, however big or small, and finding fulfillment in your daily work. When you love what you do and see how it positively affects others, that is the accurate measure of success.

Remember that while having a healthy bank balance is fantastic, it's not the be-all and end-all of business. The journey, the people you meet, the problems you solve, and the legacy you leave genuinely define the meaning of "Business is not about the dollars in your account." Embrace your entrepreneurial adventure with passion, purpose, and the intent to make the world a better place, and you'll find that the dollars in your account are just a reflection of the natural richness you've created in your life and the lives of others.

Takeaways from Empowering an Entrepreneurial Spirit

Harnessing the Entrepreneurial Spirit

This lesson inspires individuals to ignite their entrepreneurial fire, emphasizing leaping to achieve dreams. Gillian's story of transitioning from selling groundnuts to financial planning demonstrates that entrepreneurship is about making money, realizing potential, and creating opportunities. Her journey underscores the need for courage, innovation, and the determination to transform ideas into tangible success. It's a call to action for anyone harboring entrepreneurial aspirations to step forward and take their chance, knowing that the journey is rich with learning and fulfillment.

Turning Challenges into Opportunities

Gillian's transition from her initial dreams to becoming a successful entrepreneur exemplifies the power of transforming obstacles into opportunities. Her story illustrates how financial constraints and career setbacks can catalyze growth and innovation. This lesson teaches us to view challenges not as barriers but as stepping stones to new possibilities, encouraging a mindset that seeks opportunity in adversity.

Financial Independence as a Driving Force

This lesson highlights the pivotal role of financial independence in empowering entrepreneurs. Gillian's shift in focus towards securing her family's financial future showcases how entrepreneurial ventures can be more than just profit-driven. They can be motivated to provide for loved ones and create a sustainable future, emphasizing entrepreneurial success's more profound and personal rewards.

Empowering Others Through Success

Gillian's entrepreneurial journey is about personal achievement and using her success to empower others. This narrative reinforces that true entrepreneurial spirit involves lifting others as you climb and sharing success to benefit the community. It's a lesson in using one's achievements to inspire, mentor, and provide opportunities for others, thus creating a positive impact beyond individual gains.

Legacy Building Through Entrepreneurship

Finally, the concept of building a legacy through entrepreneurship. Gillian's path from selling groundnuts to financial planning is not just a story of business success; it's about creating a lasting impact. It teaches that entrepreneurship can be a means to leave a mark that extends beyond one's lifetime, impacting future generations and contributing to societal advancement. This lesson urges aspiring entrepreneurs to think long-term and consider the enduring effects of their business endeavors.

CONCLUSION

"How good and pleasant it is when God's people live together in Unity."

—Psalms 133:1

AS WE NEAR THE END of this incredible journey through *Harvesting Prosperity*, we hope you're feeling as inspired and motivated as we are. We want you to understand that the lessons and stories in this book aren't just words on paper; they are the keys to unlocking your potential and unleashing your success- harnessing your prosperity.

We've taken you on a personal journey through our life experiences and shared the profound impact of thinking positively and taking action with you. Now, we want to leave you with the key takeaways that we believe can change your life

- ❖ *Change Begins with Action*

If there's one thing that we want you to remember, it's this: change starts with action. It's always possible to take that first step towards something better. Don't just sit on the sidelines; make that move and see where it takes you.

- ❖ *A Positive Mindset is Your Superpower*

Negativity can be a heavy burden, holding you back from achieving your dreams. Embrace a positive mindset, and watch how it transforms your thinking, your actions, and, ultimately, your life. The power of positivity is a force to be reckoned with.

- ❖ *Learn from Others' Stories*

We've shared our story with you and hope it inspires you to learn from it. The world is full of stories like us about people who turned their lives around and achieved incredible things. Be open to these stories; they may contain the wisdom and inspiration you need to change your life.

- ❖ *Plan for Your Tomorrow Today*

One of the greatest lessons from this book is the importance of planning for your future. If you've realized that you haven't started planning, don't worry; start now. It's always possible to take control of your destiny and set a course for a brighter tomorrow.

Don't hesitate to reach out. We're not just the author of this book; we're here as your resource, guide, and cheerleader. Please get in touch with us if you have questions or doubts or want to discuss this further. We're here to clarify, answer, and support you on your journey to change.

As we reach the final pages of this book, we want you to know that the power to create change, turn your life around, and achieve your goals is within you. It's been a pleasure taking you on this journey, and we're excited to hear about your journey as you take action, change your mindset, and plan for a brighter future.

Remember, *Harvesting Prosperity* isn't just a catchy title; it's a truth we've explored together. It's your turn to embrace this truth, apply it to your daily life, and watch the magic happen. Your story is waiting to be written, and we can't wait to hear about the incredible changes you'll make. So, go out there, take action, and make the world your own. You've got this!

Thank you for taking this journey with us, and we can't wait to hear about the remarkable changes you'll bring into your life and those around you. Here's to a future filled with transformation, success, and the knowledge that, indeed, when we work together, change is not only possible but inevitable. Cheers to a brighter and better future!

ABOUT THE AUTHORS

GILLIAN FOMUM AND CHARLES NDAGHA are champions of change, with roots deep in the hardworking soil of Southern Cameroon's coffee farms. Gillian's resilience was forged in a family shaped by polygamy and punctuated by personal loss, leading her to advocate for financial literacy and gender equality. Charles, sharing Gillian's zeal, contributes rich experiences to their mission. Both honored graduates and influential speakers view societal advancement as a collective journey, not a solitary pursuit.

Together, they inspire action towards financial empowerment and entrepreneurial success, believing in the power of education to break the chains of poverty. *Harvesting Prosperity* is their concise guide for anyone ready to make a difference in their life and the lives of others.

www.ingramcontent.com/pod-product-compliance
Lightning Source LLC
Chambersburg PA
CBHW031316160426
43196CB00007B/562